TIGHT HIP
TWISTED CORE

TIGHT HIP
TWISTED CORE

THE KEY TO
UNRESOLVED
PAIN

CHRISTINE KOTH

Illustrated by Masha Pimas

DISCLAIMERS

This book is for informational purposes only and not intended as a substitute for the advice and care of your licensed healthcare practitioners, such as your physician or doctor. As with all health advice, please consult a doctor to make sure any recommendations in this book are appropriate for your individual circumstances. Serious or fatal injury can occur with any exercise or therapy program. This information is intended to be used for educational purposes only and implementation of these suggestions should be approved by your physician.

ISBN: 978-0-578-54292-8

Library of Congress Control Number: 2019909586

Portions of this book are works of nonfiction. Certain names and identifying characteristics have been changed. This book is not intended as a substitute for the medical advice of physicians. The reader should regularly consult a physician in matters relating to his/her health and particularly with respect to any symptoms that may require diagnosis or medical attention.

Printed in the United States of America.

www.ChristineKoth.com

A COLLECTION OF ACCOLADES FOR
TIGHT HIP, TWISTED CORE

"In her new book Tight Hip, Twisted Core, Christine uses compelling storytelling and her deep experience in physical therapy to shed light on the meaning of a 'tight hip.' She addresses an important and often dreaded twosome, what I often call the 'snarky psoas and irritated iliacus.'

As a veteran PT who specializes in hip and pelvic pain and safety for the hip in yoga, I am delighted to see Tight Hip, Twisted Core published. This much needed book can help you begin to understand some of the major players that affect hip health, and give you an understanding of what helps versus what harms the hip. Tight Hip, Twisted Core is an accessible, easy to understand text that can benefit anyone who has had hip pain or anyone whose hip is the cause of pain in other places."

Dr. Ginger Garner, DPT, ATC/L
Founder, Professional Yoga Therapy Institute®
Author of *Medical Therapeutic Yoga*
www.integrativelifestylemed.com

"If you've been everywhere and tried everything for hip, knee, ankle, or foot pain without success, read this book. Christine Koth is a talented Physical Therapist whose expertise I deeply trust. Through our years working together with patients, I've come to rely on her as the Sherlock Holmes of the team. Always striving to discover the core cause of complaints, she never stops until she finds 'the why.' Her keen eye for observation and ability to sense subtle imbalances led her to discover a major missing element to musculoskeletal complaints—the iliacus. Expanding my appreciation *for the role of this muscle has shifted my approach and improved how I manage patients with musculoskeletal pain."*

Dr. Jill Crista, Naturopathic Doctor
Best-Selling Author of *Break The Mold:
5 Tools to Conquer Mold and Take Back Your Health*
www.drcrista.com

"Christine has identified an underappreciated cause for many people suffering from hip and spinal pain. As we live in a culture where we spend most of our time in a sitting position, it is completely logical that this repetitive hip tightness is at the core of many pain conditions. When the core is twisted, the spine has no chance to be in alignment."

Dr. Noah Kaplan, D.C.,
Diplomate in Chiropractic Cranio-Cervical
Junction Procedures www.advanceuc.com

"Christine has vast knowledge and experience about this very complex and important part of our anatomy. In this book she skillfully describes the functioning, as well as the importance, of the hip flexor complex, with practical advice, tools, and examples of how to restore vitality to this area once and for all. I highly recommend this work for all healing practitioners, fitness trainers, yoga teachers, and individuals who are looking to understand the root cause of many physical and energetic discomforts in the body."

Kristen Dessange
MS Biology, Yoga Teacher of 15 years,
Founder of Sacred Life Circle LLC
www.SacredLifeCircle.com

"Christine Koth understands the complex dynamics of the hip and with her tools brings relief to those who suffer. I've witnessed this both in my own body and in my patients during the decades of working side by side with her. This book teaches how to effectively treat a tight hip and twisted core, exposing why the hip flexor complex is important, why it gets tight,

what happens to the entire body when it is tight, and what to do about it. It is a valuable tool for those who suffer, as well as health care providers."

Dr. Allison Becker, ND, LAc
www.doctorallisonbecker.com

"I am astounded by Christine's ability to clearly articulate this mysterious concept in a way that anyone can understand it. This is a huge discovery in how the hip area works, and how one tight muscle affects the rest of the body. This book will significantly impact the way health care professionals treat the hip from now on."

Zach Renner, Crossfit Trainer
Former College Athlete
Founder of Awakened Athlete
www.awakenedathlete.com

FOREWORD

For those who are constantly stretching out their hips but getting no relief or don't see how their hips could possibly be connected to their pain in other places, get ready to have your mind blown.

It takes an unusually holistic physical therapist like Christine Koth to take the subject of the previously little-known iliacus muscle and make it rock-star sexy in her new book, *Tight Hip, Twisted Core*. Patients and practitioners alike will love this "hip tome" she has created covering the what, where, why, and HOW to unlock that hip and finally release your unresolved pain.

The truth is that the iliacus is not a focus in medical schooling and often just lumped together with the psoas, which is also deeply discussed. As you'll see in Koth's book, that tight iliacus creates a host of unmitigated body misalignment, unhappy patients, and frustrated practitioners.

There's a little secret that very few in the public know—your body will always fight to keep your eyes level with the horizon. That means that if your hip is rotated, your body will twist your spine to the other direction and lean your head in an effort to get your eyes or vision level with the world around you. This is why the consequence of a tight iliacus can be felt anywhere in the body, from a headache to plantar fasciitis in your feet.

Koth does an excellent job of addressing why you want to get to the *root cause* of your pain and not just treat the symptoms. In fact, doing so might numb some pain but also turn off the warning signal that is your body screaming for attention. Solve the problem, don't just mute the pain.

Read the book. You'll learn why. You'll learn how. You'll find relief. Tight hips no more!

Rock on,
Dr. Brandy Zachary, DC, ACN
Body Love Cafe
Doctor of Chiropractic, Functional Medicine Practitioner

TABLE OF CONTENTS

TIGHT HIP

TWISTED CORE

INTRODUCTION

"You can't see what you don't know is there."
All we know is what we know. Those things we have never been taught about ourselves continue to be a mystery until one day they are brought into view. If you've never been taught about what's inside your body and how it works, what's behind the scenes, those parts inside of you might as well not even be there.

Real solutions present themselves only when you know the true cause. When you are missing a piece of the puzzle, the problem will not be solved, at least not permanently. Try putting together a table when you only have three of the four legs. It may stand for a moment but as soon as the wind blows, the table falls over. Try curing diabetes without changing the diet. A medication may lessen the symptoms but the disease will still be there. Try driving a car without aligning the wheels. It might drive for a while but eventually, it will break down.

The point is, you need to know the "why" to solve the problem. For decades, this has been my mission as a holistic physical therapist, to find and remedy the true cause. *The* reason for many different injuries and areas of pain is revealed to you upon these pages. Mysteriously, this undiscovered source of pain is hidden in plain sight and is not being treated in millions of people. This simply obvious obstacle to living a pain-free life is easy to remove but remains unrecognized by most people and healers. Together we are about to unearth this sacred nugget of truth about how your body works. Together we will find out the source of *your* pain too.

It's time to illuminate the importance of an undiscovered muscle that is deep inside your core (abdominal and hip region). It has been hidden here from your time in the womb, quietly doing its job every moment of every day. It has grown up underappreciated and ignored. Its loud and bossy sibling undeservingly gets all the attention.

(*drum roll*) Please welcome to the stage the muscle that you didn't know existed, that helps you walk, sit, and play. It is tight in almost everyone for many different reasons, causing pain from head to toe, but very few people even know it exists. Meet "Silly Yak Kiss!" (*applause*)

Iliacus rhymes with "Silly Yak Kiss"

Actually, its official name is the iliacus (pronounced "illy ak us") muscle, but to help you remember it, it rhymes with "Silly Yak Kiss." Medical terms can be a pain (pun intended) but I really want you to know this muscle intimately so you can call it by its first name. Then you can joke at a family gathering about your iliacus. You can bring your iliacus to the attention of your doctor. You can even sing an iliacus chant as you do your Sunday chores. This muscle is so important it needs to become a household name. By reading this book you are one of the first to master this muscle. Soon you won't be so alone. We can all use more "Silly Yak Kiss" in our lives.

In my professional opinion, the iliacus is *the* most undertreated and underappreciated muscle of the body. Most people don't even know that the iliacus exists, let alone what it does to impact the body and how it keeps you out of pain, but that's about to change.

During my many years of working with clients, I have yet to have even one person tell me they have had their iliacus treated before coming to me. Not one! This pattern of the iliacus being ignored, when it is such a vitally important part of our body, is my motivation for this book. After countless successes releasing the iliacus and zero evidence that this muscle is being widely addressed by anyone else, I've come to this conclusion. It's time for a shift in perspective. There are so many people who are struggling and aren't getting better because they are not addressing the actual cause of their pain. The answer is right there, hidden right around the corner on the inside surface of the pelvic bone.

You may have heard of the hip flexor, a more commonly known term. Hip flexion is actually describing a type of motion. This motion moves the whole leg forward at the hip, as in walking or marching. Any muscle that helps do this motion is called a "hip flexor." There are actually many muscles that could be considered hip flexors. However, when a layperson uses the words "hip flexor" they are typically referring to the two largest hip flexors in the body, the iliacus and the psoas (pronounced "so as"). When grouped together they can also be called iliopsoas (pronounced "illy o so as"). Although commonly called the hip flexor, we will use iliopsoas throughout this book to more accurately describe these two muscles when referred to together.

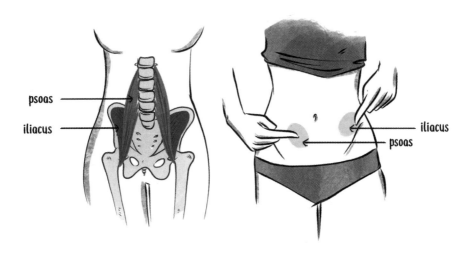

Location of iliacus and psoas in the body

Psoas in the Limelight

Professionals in the field of medicine and fitness give the psoas a lot more attention then the iliacus. Indeed, the psoas is very large, it takes up a lot of space, and its job is very central to keeping the upper body connected to the lower body and keeping the core of our body working properly. The core is the central part of your body where the spine, pelvis, and hips intersect and where all movements begin. The psoas muscle does get very tight from being overused with too much sitting, for example—many of the same reasons the iliacus gets tight as well. Although some healthcare professionals do address the psoas, very few put any attention on the iliacus. This misses a major cause of issues in this area of the body. Now is the time to give the iliacus its due respect and time on the stage. It is a star in the show, but for some odd reason, the psoas is always in the limelight. No longer! The iliacus is coming out of the closet as the underappreciated sibling that has been doing all the work behind the scenes and getting no attention. The iliacus is screaming for help and recognition.

Because the iliacus is the next-door neighbor, and the true companion to the psoas, some people assume because they work on their psoas that they're addressing the iliacus as well. This is false. These are two separate muscles and they are located in two nearby, but separate, locations. Working on the psoas does not, by default, fix the iliacus. Just because it shares the same attachment point with the psoas does not mean that they should be grouped as one. In fact, I've repeatedly seen people who have had temporary relief after working on their psoas muscle find long-lasting relief once their iliacus was also addressed.

Very few physical therapists, chiropractors, doctors, massage therapists, or personal trainers have been trained to see the importance of the iliacus separate from the psoas muscle and therefore, most don't address it all. When mentioning the importance of the iliacus, a colleague of mine recently asked, "Why not just treat the psoas? Isn't it the same thing?" Needless to say, it is overlooked in a lot of treatment protocols and a lot of athletic endeavors, mistakenly grouped with the psoas.

The location of the iliacus muscle is right on the inside surface of the pelvis and it's a hard muscle to reach on your own. Whereas the psoas is more accessible, the iliacus is hidden. This may be why it has been ignored for so long. The reality is that the iliacus can be found and treated quite simply with the special techniques taught in this book. Now anyone can know and treat their own iliacus muscle and experience the exquisite transformation of the body that naturally follows.

Building Blocks of the Body

Each part of our body has a role. The bones support your body and the joints are where the bones connect. Joints allow the body to move but the bones wouldn't move at all if it weren't for the muscles. Muscles are attached to the bones by tendons so that they can contract and move those bones around, so you can do your thing. If it weren't for the ligaments and joint capsules holding the joints together, those movable connections of one bone to another would fall apart as soon as the muscle tried to move them. Then there is the fascia, which runs continuously from head to toe. Fascia holds the muscles, cells, organs, nerves, all parts of the body, in place. If you didn't have fascia, your muscles would be hanging off the bone.

When one part of the body is too tight or too loose or broken or weak, it affects the way the rest of the body works. Since each bone is connected to the next by this network of ligaments, tendons, and muscles, when part of the system is not working well, it impacts the rest of the body. We see this when a broken toe leads to back pain or when knee surgery creates a hip problem.

The Chain Reaction

An unhealthy iliacus has profound effects on the rest of the body. Due to the location and strength of the iliacus and how it connects to both the pelvis and the thigh bone, it is involved in issues with the low back, tailbone, hip, leg, knee, foot, toe, upper body, and neck. Because its tightness twists the core and changes the way the leg is connected to the upper body, all of these areas are affected. When the iliacus is relaxed and happy, these areas have a chance to work as they have been designed to work—with ease, aligned and strong. When the iliacus is tight, all of these areas are susceptible to pain and injury.

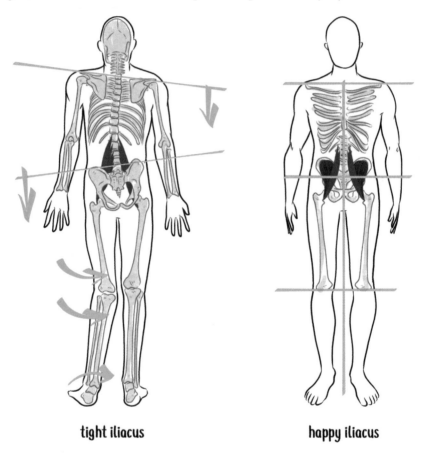

tight iliacus   happy iliacus

A tight hip twists the core, affecting the entire body

Tightness in the iliacus is caused by either overuse (sitting too long or certain athletic endeavors) or by a too flexible body (where the muscles have to hold on for dear life to keep the body from falling apart). Injuries and stress contribute as well. Once this tightness sets in, it can persist for years, pulling on the pelvis and creating a faulty movement pattern in the leg to the toe and the spine to the head. That strain starts to wear away at the body, usually at your weakest link, and eventually leads to the one thing that no one wants and everyone wants to get rid of: pain. The iliacus is commonly the root cause of a chain of events that leads to pain; therefore, if we keep our iliacus healthy and happy, we can simply avoid so much suffering.

Become a part of this movement by intimately knowing your iliacus and how to take care of it. Get on the iliacus train to your own wellness and evolve into a better functioning you. Soon you will be an expert on how to care for this muscle, and your newfound knowledge will help to create a world where ***everyone knows they have an iliacus, its importance, how to care for it, and lives pain-free.***

Discovering the Iliacus

Upon emerging from the womb I've been curiously examining the world around me, looking around wide-eyed from the shoulder of my mother in amazement and asking "why" from the moment I could speak. I have fond memories as a young child of sitting in the grass and writing lists of questions for which I, at that time, could not find an answer. Everything was a mystery to me that I knew I could solve. At the sweet age of four, I would run to my aunt at any chance I could get. She would sit with me for hours, as any good kindergarten teacher would, and let me ask her my "why" questions. "Why can insects fly and humans cannot? Why do we have two nostrils for a nose? How will I ever understand it all?" It's no surprise that I was drawn to science.

It's easy now, in retrospect, to see the clear path to this iliacus discovery: from the inquisitive nature and tenacity I was born with, to the way I was somehow able to see the forest for the trees while noticing the microscopic wonder of the moss that methodically and uniquely grows on each and every branch. I still hike with my magnifying glass and I'm simultaneously drawn to the most majestic of vistas, viewing this complex and yet so simple world with amazement.

Zooming in, I studied biochemistry as an undergraduate, learning which molecule did what. Zooming out, I finished my master's in physical therapy (MPT) degree, studying how the body works as a whole and seeing how each part of the whole impacted the rest. Fascinating. All of it. Even after decades of pondering this amazing body we live in and the wildly fascinating world we experience with it, I'm still asking "why," finding the gaps in my understanding bit by bit.

I graduated from physical therapy school at the top of my class, understanding how the body works from books, but still asking myself, "How am I going to be able to feel these structures with my hands?" I could see a muscle in the pictures in my textbook and imagine where it was under the skin during my internships as a young clinician, but I willfully hoped that someday I'd develop the skills for my hands to *feel* it too. Who knew that I'd soon be known to have "magic hands" that would be able to zero in on an issue far faster than my mind could comprehend it?

I was fortunate enough when I graduated from college to get a job because the physical therapy market was very competitive at the time. I was determined to find a job in an outpatient clinic, so I paged through the phone book and called all of the physical therapy clinics that were near my first apartment out of college. One such clinic, only fifteen minutes away, answered the phone. It was just my luck that they were just starting to consider looking for a physical therapist. It felt like it was meant to be. As soon as I got off the phone, I slipped into my shoes and quickly drove to my first (and only) interview out of college. Upon arrival, the professional sign towering over the building and shadow of exercise equipment and treatment tables seen through the window brought a hint of that "first day of the rest of my life" kind of feeling. Little did I know that this clinic was going to start me on my path to having "magic hands" and being an iliacus P.T.G. (Physical Therapy Geek), a self-proclaimed acronym we used in college for getting excited about PT things.

The hiring process unfolded with ease and I immersed myself in the unique hands-on philosophy of the clinic. These kinds of clinics were an anomaly (they still are, unfortunately). Most physical therapy clinics are more exercise-based or use machines. These are effective tools for rehabilitation but some people need human touch to heal and that can't be delivered by a machine. Melody, the owner of this glorious company that graciously hired me, was breaking the mold.

All of the PTs working at this clinic were trained in manual therapies. So many of them had been trained in techniques like myofascial release (releasing the adhesions in connective tissue with gentle pressure), craniosacral therapy (guiding the bones in the skull to move well so that spinal fluid can bathe the brain), and trigger point release (prolonged pressure to a muscle to decrease its tension). More importantly, they were encouraged to use the healing power of touch to treat their clients every day, and hours and hours of touching people gives you an understanding of the body that you cannot gain from any book. Some of the practitioners had been working there for twenty or thirty years, and luckily my fresh and bushy-tailed, newly graduated self got to learn from them.

As I oriented to this new job, I was taken under the wings of these seasoned physical therapists. Janet would show me how to cradle the head without digging my nails into the skin and how to get a good enough grip to actually stretch the neck. Jessie watched my hand placement when releasing the chest muscle and then asked me, "Did you feel that?" David would invite me in to see his clients with him, letting them experience a "two for the price of one" session while I started to put the pieces together. In between clients the therapists would compare my observations with theirs. We also got together as a group once a month to share new tools that we had learned and practice on each other. Soon I was actually feeling what's inside the body with my hands and not having to imagine it solely with my mind.

One of the very first techniques that I learned was a psoas release. This technique involves pressure on a muscle to get it to relax. If you look on your own abdomen and you draw a line from your belly button to the front of your right hip bone, somewhere in there lies your psoas muscle. It's not necessarily an easy muscle to get to. Although I was getting better at feeling muscles and bones with my hands, this one was a tough one. It's deep inside, there are a lot of other things in the abdomen, and touching someone there was a bit more intimate than I was used to.

David patiently showed me the technique, how to find the muscle, and where to look between the belly button and the hip. He let me put my hand on his abdomen and clumsily feel around and try to see if I could find it. Laying down, David lifted his leg up to contract the psoas and, lo and behold, I was actually touching the psoas. I could feel it pressing against my fingers.

I decided to take advantage of David's offer to let me continue feeling around his abdomen. I tried over and over again, finding and pressing on the psoas muscle, looking at my anatomy book opened to the side of us, continuing to visualize what's actually happening in the body as I'm feeling around. Exploring closer to the pelvic bone itself, I notice some tightness there too. It feels like there's another muscle there. Based on the page open in my book, it looked like the iliacus muscle. Hmmm. Interesting. As I pressed on that muscle David sighed—"That's a good spot"—and after a few minutes of trembling novice fingers trying to maintain the pressure, the muscle softened. David got off the table with a "That was great!" I kept a mental note of that moment.

As I started treating clients I was on the prowl for the source of their pain. That inborn inquisitiveness kept me searching for *the* reason why they were having pain. For example, if a client came in with knee pain, yes, I'd treat the knee, but I wanted to look deeper. Why did they develop knee pain in the first place? I would examine the alignment of the body when sitting, standing, and walking. It became standard practice to feel around in the tissues of the body, as I had been trained. Those meandering hands have come to know a lot of bodies in my decades of practice.

Working with more and more people I started noticing that not only do many have a tight psoas but also a tight iliacus. Because I was a novice, and a little cautious about digging into somebody's abdomen, I tended to release the iliacus muscle first because it was a little more accessible—it was right near the bone, not deep in the abdomen. I didn't have to manipulate any organs to get to the iliacus—it just felt easier. It became my go-to technique when I wasn't so comfortable with my hands yet. I soon noticed that, as I was releasing the tension in the iliacus and completely ignoring the psoas, people were getting better without any attention to the psoas at all.

The technique to release the iliacus I developed during this time and I still use it to this day. Because I was new at using my hands, I hadn't quite figured out how to use my body mechanics in a way that would keep me from hurting myself working on clients all day. As I left the office each day, wrapping my hands in ice and taping my fingers together to keep them strong, I knew this kind of abuse on my hands was not sustainable. My technique was awkward at first. I couldn't figure out the table height or how to place my body in a way that would protect me from harm. My mind was solving the problems that faced my clients while trying to determine how I could survive a full day of using my hands with clients without hurting *myself*.

When releasing the iliacus, originally, I was approaching the muscle from the same side of the body. If I were treating the right side I was standing on the right side of the person and putting my hands into the body. After many awkward attempts and inability to really apply a decent amount of pressure at a good angle, I decided to go to the left side of the body to reach across the abdomen for the right iliacus. I realized in that moment how much more effective it was to pin the muscle up against the bone and release the tension that way. It was much easier on my body and way more effective, so it was a no-brainer to make that technique my standard method for releasing the iliacus.

Discovering a tight iliacus in so many of my clients and the newly modified technique of releasing that muscle was resulting in happy and healed customers. Over time, I started to notice how this muscle was impacting so many different parts of the body. Over decades of practice I have seen so many different conditions, everything from bunions to knee arthritis to hip arthritis to back pain to tailbone joint problems. As I would evaluate a new client and assess their whole body and not just focus on the part that was hurting, inevitably, many had tight iliacus muscles. Miraculously, as I released the tension in that muscle, their pain got better.

I remember the office doorbell ringing as Kendra entered in her mesh running shorts and New Balance shoes, carrying her handbag filled with English papers to grade and a folded-up training plan for her next marathon. She thought her life was over when she couldn't run anymore because of knee pain. The tattered brace on her knee hinted at defeat in the same way that she plopped herself onto the treatment table. She reminded me of myself as a kid, with the same list of a million questions she wanted answered. She started drilling this rookie PT with curious observations about her knee. "My kneecap is *killing* me when I run even three miles," she sighed with defeat. She went on to share all the details, including a conversation about sleep. "I have to put two pillows under my knees in order to fall asleep," she recalled. "It's not so much for my knees but I can't lie flat without the pillow under my knees or my back will hurt!" Interesting.

I had her lie on the treatment table to show me her pillow configurations. When I took the pillows out from underneath her, she was so tight in her hips that she couldn't lie flat at all. She needed those pillows under her knees to take the tension off her extremely tight iliopsoas so her back wouldn't be strained while sleeping. With standing, the side where she was having her knee pain was rotated forward at her pelvis, twisting her core. This tightness in her iliopsoas was affecting her entire leg! Her thigh bone was rotated inward and didn't line up with her kneecap, causing rubbing and much pain, all because of her tight iliopsoas.

We went right to work on her iliopsoas, focusing on the iliacus muscle as I knew best, standing on her left side to reach over her abdomen to skillfully press on that tight right iliacus muscle. She came for treatment three times a week and after a few weeks of getting that muscle to relax, teaching it how to stop being constantly contracted, the alignment of her pelvis started to equalize. With a few exercises and lifestyle shifting tips, she was free of her knee pain for good and back to running as she had done before her pain had stopped her.

Years went by and then one day this email arrived.

"How are you, Christine? I have a question for you. Will you send me a list of the things that you and David did to treat me ten years ago? I'm on my second physical therapist where I live now and I'm tired of messing around. All I know is whatever you and David did to me worked; it changed my life. I did not know that it was possible to feel so good. I want to get back to that place of no pain. I remember you releasing the hip by pushing in my abdomen. I remember doing exercises but forget exactly which ones I did. I'm grateful for your help, not only for relieving my pain, but for showing me that there is a plan that can work for me out there. Your plan worked."

This is one of many such communications I have received from past clients. Clients continue to arrive at my office after having been to multiple other practitioners without results, all because they ignore the impact of the iliacus on their pain. As you can see, with Kendra and many others I've treated, giving proper attention to the iliacus is vital to the pain-free lifestyle we all desire.

Kendra contacted me fifteen years after her initial appointment to share her testimonial. This says it all:

"I think Christine is one of the greatest things on Earth. I have her on one of my top five positively influential people in my life. I did not know one could be without pain until I learned from Christine at age 32."

This beautiful story is just one of many that have been a catalyst for my work in figuring out how important this muscle is in the body. I'm honored to share all that I have learned with you so that you too can easily determine the cause of your pain and fix it for good.

Hip Hook

After moving my family and physical therapy practice from Wisconsin to California, I left many loyal clients behind without access to my magic hands to release their tight iliacus, untwist their core, and resolve their pain.

I experimented with various balls, rollers, and household items in an attempt to find a way for my clients to self-release the iliacus, but the results were subpar to my fingers. It was impossible to get to the right spot at the right angle with the right force.

In 2019, I took it upon myself to design a better solution. By replicating the exact angle, pressure, and location that my fingers had mastered in the form of a tool that people could use on their own, the Hip Hook was born. Designed specifically to release the iliacus, the

Hip Hook allows you to resolve your pain that is caused by a tight hip and twisted core without the help of a practitioner.

How to Use this Book

This book is designed to give you the information that is pertinent to you and your situation so that you can quickly identify what the iliacus muscle is, why it might be tight in you, what happens to your body when it is tight, and what to do about it. By reading *Tight Hip, Twisted Core* in its entirety, you'll get a deep understanding of the role of this muscle in your life and how to take good care of it. Feel free to skip around to find tidbits that speak to you directly.

"Part 1: Setting the Stage," gives a brief overview of the hip and pelvic area to orient the iliacus muscle in the environment in which it lives. Also in this section, "I'm So Tight!" shares specifics about what it means to be tight and how tightness even occurs. This is key information that everyone needs to know about the body, exposing many myths. "Part 2: Why Is My Hip So Tight?" lists the many ways that a tight iliacus and psoas develop, giving you an explanation for how you may have arrived at having a tight hip in the first place. "Part 3: A Tight Hip Twists the Core," describes the effect of a tight iliacus and psoas on the rest of the body. This is where the tight hip as a cause of various pains is explained.

The next section, "Part 4: Soften the Hip to Solve Your Pain," starts with a quiz to help you determine if you have a tight iliacus and which side is tightest. Then the fun part: you get to learn the "3 Simple Steps" to release the tension in your hip and align your pelvis. Finally, unveiled in "Keep the Iliacus Relaxed," you will learn strategies for living your life *and* keeping the iliacus and psoas happy.

PART 1:
SETTING THE STAGE

To know the iliacus, you must understand where it lives. Its home is arguably the most important part of the body and therefore the iliacus is involved in much more than meets the eye.

Zooming in you can see how very close the iliacus and psoas muscles are to the hip joint, the pelvis, and the spine. It's not hard to imagine how important these muscles are to holding this area together. When you look really closely at where both the psoas and the iliacus attach to the thigh bone, you'll see these muscles literally lay on top of the hip joint itself. No wonder they are so closely related to the hip!

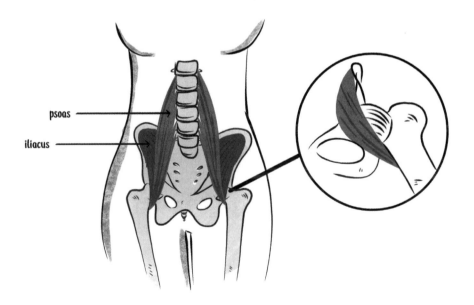

The attachment of the iliacus and psoas is extremely
close to the hip joint

15

Whenever we have muscles that are really close to a joint they often act as stabilizers. The psoas, with its connection to the spine, works hard to keep the lower spine stable, and the iliacus, with its connection to the pelvis and hip, puts a lot of effort into stabilizing the hip joint and SI (sacroiliac) joint. The SI joint is underneath the bony dimples on the back of the body where the tailbone connects to the pelvis. The iliopsoas is really holding together the foundation of it all.

It's a big job being responsible for connecting the upper body to the lower body. An oak seed must be firmly planted in the soil for the roots to take hold and the shoots to sprout from the earth, allowing the tree to withstand wind and erosion alike. Similarly, the pelvis must be firmly stabilized for the spine to sprout and the legs to move about. If the iliacus and psoas are not working properly, the foundation of the body is not settled in the soil properly. The result: the body is weak and wobbly as it sprouts up to our tilted head and roots down to our crooked feet.

This area, often referred to as the core, is responsible for a lot of the essential functions of the body. All of our reproduction, bowel and bladder action, and digestion happens in this space, right next to the iliopsoas. The ability to sit, squat, and do almost everything starts at the core. Other areas have their vital roles too, but if things are not functioning well in the core, it's easy to imagine the train wreck that can ensue.

Let's take a closer look at this magical place where the iliacus lives. The iliacus and psoas are holding the story all together; they have been cast as the lead parts in this play. They act in the most dynamic of stages with huge bony puppets that they move around. Other muscles share the stage and act as the Villains and Sidekicks. Let's take a peek at how this adventurous scene plays out.

The Stage

The iliacus and psoas play the leading role on a stage full of commotion. Like the streets of New York City, there is a lot going on all around these muscles as they are smooshed in the crowd. Living amongst friends and foes, the iliacus and psoas play their role on a jam-packed stage, just trying to do their job of moving and stabilizing the hip, pelvis, and spine.

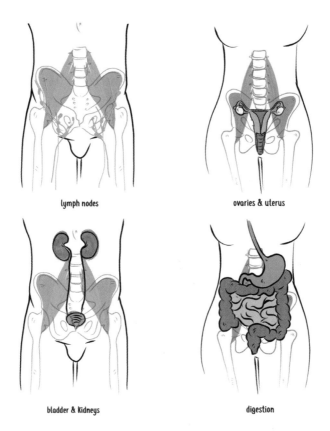

lymph nodes   ovaries & uterus

bladder & kidneys   digestion

Many of our internal organs lie adjacent to the iliacus and psoas

- First, the lymph system, strung like lights around the stage. It clears toxins, excess fluid, and waste from the space in between the cells and dumps it back into the bloodstream. It's a big part of our immune system, helping to kill foreign invaders and clean up the rubble from the fight. Right in front of the hip joint, in the groin area, there are some major lymph nodes, working hard to do the job of clean-up.

- The parts of the body responsible for reproduction and urination are a part of the stage that is the core. Issues with the kidney and bladder and with the reproductive organs can affect how this play evolves and how the iliopsoas speaks its lines. Big scenes like pregnancy or an ovarian cyst can really impact these muscles. The ovaries, uterus, and bladder are all intimately connected to the hip joint and the pelvis.

- Digestion is rumbling away all day long on this stage. It's definitely the sound system. The small intestine and the large intestine are right next to the iliacus and psoas. Issues with these tissues can definitely affect what's happening in the muscles and vice versa. It's quite a community.

- The nerves are the electrical wiring on the stage. There are tons of nerves that travel through the pelvic area as they come out of the spine; the iliacus and the psoas have to navigate around them. They don't want to trip on a wire!

- Major arteries and veins make up the plumbing of the stage, showing how circulation is a part of the play too.

When the stage isn't functioning properly, the actors and the puppets can't play out the scene as planned. If you have digestive, urinary, reproductive, lymph, or nerve issues, the iliopsoas will be affected. And issues with the iliopsoas will affect those tissues as well. It's quite a complex set on a lively, crowded stage.

Bones as the Puppets

Now that we've set the stage for what happens around the iliacus and psoas, let's explore the bony puppets. The bones are called the puppets because the muscles grab a hold of the bones, like the strings of a puppet, and move them around to get the body to move. The bones are inanimate; they will not move alone, just like a puppet. The bones need the muscles to move them.

The main puppets in this show are the thigh bone (femur), pelvis, and spine (vertebrae). The thigh bone connects to the pelvic bone to make up the hip joint. The pelvis itself is made up of three bones, two (called the ilium) that join in the front to make the pubic joint. Both of those bones connect on the back to the tailbone (sacrum) to create the SI (sacroiliac) joints.

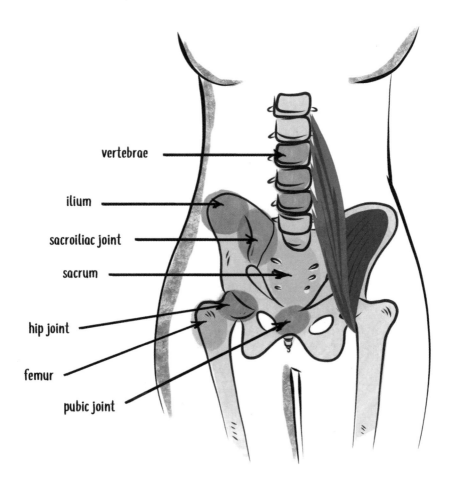

vertebrae

ilium

sacroiliac joint

sacrum

hip joint

femur

pubic joint

The bones and joints around the iliopsoas muscles

The iliacus crosses over the hip joint, attaches directly to the pelvis, and affects the SI joint. The psoas crosses over both the hip joint and the pelvis all the way to the spine. Moving and holding together these puppets, the iliacus and the psoas have a big job to do—these bones are pretty important for getting around and being upright. Balancing mobility and stability of this area is hard work!

Muscles as the Actors

There are nineteen muscles that cross the hip joint, two being the iliacus and psoas. Each muscle crosses the joint at different angles. Some are very long, going from the pelvis to the knee, while others are just a few inches in length. All of these muscles have their own role in the play, either working with the iliopsoas or in opposition to it.

The Stars

The stage has been set, the puppets are in place, now it's time to welcome to the stage the stars of the show: Iliacus and Psoas. Crossing from the lower back to attach to the thigh bone, they are in every scene played out on the stage, speaking their lines loud and proud.

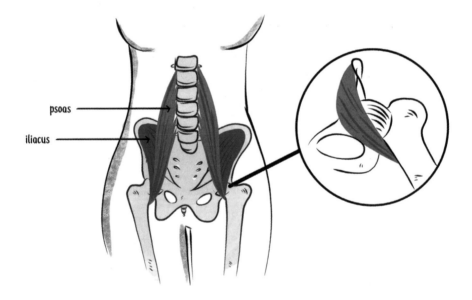

Iliacus and psoas are intimately connected to the spine,
pelvis, and hip joint

The iliacus holds on to the inside of the pelvis bone, comes down the front of the hip, and connects to the front of the thigh bone. It's *very* close to the hip joint itself. If you could peer inside the body you would see that the end of the iliacus (and the psoas) actually touch the outside edge of the hip joint, super close. The psoas starts with its connective tissue attachment to the diaphragm and then a tight grip on the entire lower spine. Finally it attaches to the same spot in front of the hip as the iliacus, on the front of the thigh bone.

The role of these two muscles is twofold. First, they help flex the hip. Remember, hip flexion is when you're moving your leg forward with your hip joint. When you lift your leg to place your foot upon a stair you're partially using your iliopsoas. When you swing your leg forward in walking, running, or kicking, you're using your iliopsoas. Imagine what happens to these muscles when they are working too hard. They get kinda cranky like anyone whose name is constantly called all day long.

The second and most important role of these two muscles is to hold the spine in a good position relative to the pelvis, and to hold the pelvis and spine in a good position relative to the hip joint. The body works best when the spine, pelvis, and hip are all lined up nicely and held together snuggly. The iliacus and psoas act like the rubber bands that hold the stack of cards together, connecting the upper body to the lower body. From the spine the upper body springs; from the hips, the lower body trickles. Without healthy iliacus and psoas muscles this area wouldn't line up right and could possibly topple out of place.

As they are acting on this crowded stage inside the abdomen, deep in the body, you may be wondering how we can find the iliacus and psoas muscles in all that traffic. I think the commotion actually deters a lot of people from paying too much attention to these muscles because they seem like they are too hard to reach.

There also exists some sort of a cultural sensitivity that makes people cautious about working on the abdomen. In other cultures, this is not the case. Similarly, when you don't understand an area, it's hard to jump in and treat it, just like I felt as a new graduate. Regardless of the reason why, the truth is that these muscles are easily accessible, especially the iliacus. The iliacus and the psoas can be massaged, released, and touched to see if they are happy. (Happy muscles don't hurt.)

The iliacus performs on stage right and left and a little in the wings. On your body, it's a bit around the corner, on the inside surface of the pelvic bone, partially hidden. But that doesn't mean you can't touch it. It just requires a little creativity.

Since the psoas performs between stage right and left and center stage, you can see why it's natural that psoas gets all the attention. Many assume the psoas is the star of the show because it's so big and loud and in the center of the stage! Little do they know that the script will fall apart without the role of the iliacus firmly in the wings.

Take a moment to explore how this plays out in your own body. If you put your hands on your hips you can feel your pelvic bones. The deep crease in the front of your hip is the location of the hip joint and the attachment of the iliacus and psoas. So if you're experiencing symptoms in the crease it could be related to iliacus, psoas, or the hip joint itself.

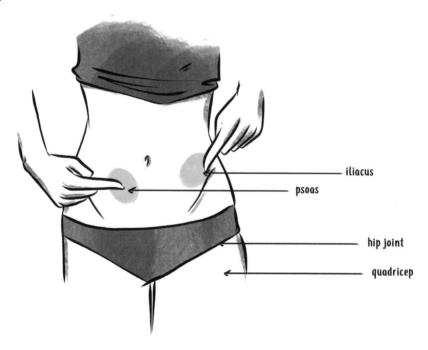

Find these spots on *your* body

The iliacus starts in that spot right in the inner crease of the hip and attaches on the inner surface of the pelvic bone. If you put your hands on your hips and you feel the bony point on the front of the pelvis and you go to the soft spot just a little bit towards your belly button, that's where the bulk of your iliacus lives. Draw a line halfway from your belly button to that bony point on the front of the pelvis to find your psoas.

The iliacus and the psoas are the well-deserved co-stars of the show. After all, they are holding the whole thing together. They both need your attention. Let's explore the muscles that act as the Sidekicks and hold supporting roles to iliopsoas.

The Sidekicks

These Sidekick muscles, like those in the starring role, have a similar job bringing the leg forward, so they tend to commiserate with an angry iliopsoas muscle.

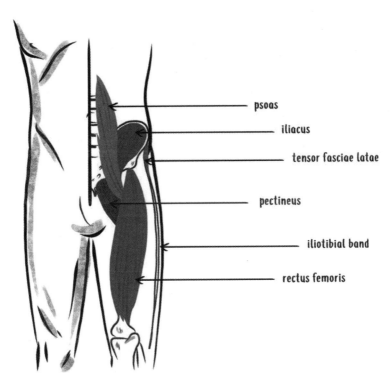

psoas

iliacus

tensor fasciae latae

pectineus

iliotibial band

rectus femoris

Other major hip flexors acting as Sidekicks to the iliopsoas
(gluteus medius and sartorius not shown)

Pectineus (peck-ti-knee-us) is in the inner thigh. Rectus femoris is part of our quadricep, the big muscle on the front of the thigh. Tensor fasciae latae (ten-sir fash-ha lot-a), one of my all-time favorite names for a muscle, attaches to the IT (iliotibial) band on the outside of your leg. Part of the gluteus medius, located on the outside of the hip, also supports the iliopsoas. All of these muscles are hip flexors and support the iliacus and psoas in their starring role.

These Sidekicks are just as important to the plot of the story because when there are issues with the iliacus or the psoas, these Sidekick muscles are also not so happy. They may be overworked, they may be sore, they may be tight and pulling on the bony puppets in their own way, so they too need attention.

The Villains

The stage has been set, the puppets are in place, the stars of the show and the newly introduced Sidekicks have entered stage left…just in time for the Villains to arrive. The Villains are the muscles that fight with the hip flexor muscles. These Villains are not necessarily bad, they just have the opposite job of the iliopsoas and the Sidekicks. Their role is just as important.

This tug-of-war is how the body moves so elegantly. One group of muscles pulls one way while the opposing muscles pull the opposite direction, both attempting to keep the bones in place. When the iliacus and psoas are pulling too much, the Villains activate to keep the iliopsoas from winning. Since the hip flexors are on the front of the body to pull the leg forward, the Villains are mostly in the back of the body.

The gluteus maximus and minimus (often called the glute) help pull the leg backward. Quadratus lumborum and low back muscles get cramped and tight when the iliopsoas is tight. The hamstring muscle, attaching directly to the pelvis, plays a mean game of tug-of-war with a tight iliacus. Joining the game, deeper in the pelvis, lives the piriformis muscle. The sciatic nerve runs right underneath it, so when piriformis plays tug-of-war, that nerve is affected.

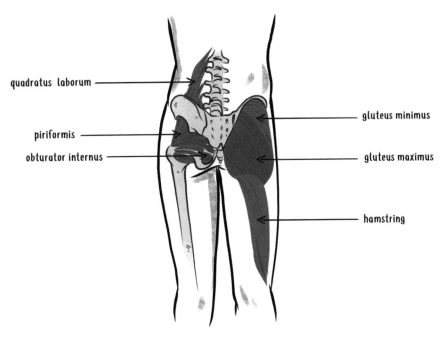

quadratus laborum

gluteus minimus

piriformis

obturator internus

gluteus maximus

hamstring

Villians of the iliopsoas on the back of the body that like to play tug-of-war

The obturator internus muscle is another undertreated and undiscovered muscle deep in the pelvis that is quite tight in a lot of people who have tight iliopsoas. This muscle is really close to the back part of the hip joint, similar to how the iliopsoas is close to the front part of the hip joint. They are definitely tugging on each other. The obturator internus and the iliacus are often tight together with issues with the hip joint and the pelvic floor. Obturator internus is part of a larger group of muscles called the deep hip rotators. Similarly, these muscles are really close to the back of the hip joint and therefore become Villains in the show.

The Villains in this show fight with the iliacus and psoas to be in the spotlight. If the Villains are overworked or tight, that might contribute to the cause of why the hip flexors are tight to begin with. Alternatively, if the hip flexors are tight, these Villain muscles are going to play tug-of-war and can get inflamed or tight as a result.

Take a moment to explore the Villains on the back of your own body. The part of the thigh bone that is on the outside of the hip (greater trochanter) is where a lot of the Villains attach, like the deep hip rotators, glute, and piriformis. This bone can hurt when those muscles are angry.

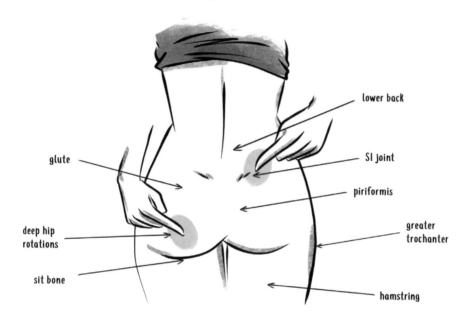

lower back

SI joint

piriformis

glute

greater trochanter

deep hip rotations

sit bone

hamstring

Find these spots on *your* body

Following the hip crests to the back of the pelvis, you find two bony knobs that may look like dimples. This is where the pelvic bone (ilium) and the tailbone (sacrum) connect. This is the SI (sacroiliac) joint, near where the other end of the piriformis attaches. The lower back starts in the center between those two bony points. To the side of the tailbone in the soft fleshy part is the bulk of the Villain muscles.

On the back of the thigh is the hamstring muscle. If you sit down on a chair and you put your hands under your bottom you will find two bony points, the "sit" bones, where the hamstring attaches. Moving your fingertips to the inside surface of the sit bones, you'll find the obturator internus, and the space in between the sit bones is the pelvic floor, full of muscles waiting to get tight.

Now consider yourself oriented to the stage, puppets, and the actors in the greatest show on earth, playing live right now in your core. Let's see how the story is scripted and how you can start to run the show.

"I'm So Tight!"

How many times have you thought to yourself, "My (fill in the blank) is so tight!" As a result of athletic endeavors or a long day at the office, we are bound to feel something we call "tight" at some point. This word is used prolifically in conversation and exclamation, sometimes to even explain a vague and undefined sensation. This book is about the effect of tightness of the iliacus muscle on the rest of the body; therefore, it's key that we get the definition of "tight" straight.

Not Really "Tight"

"Tight" is commonly used for more meanings than there are shades of green. One person might explain a certain feeling as "tight" even though another person's description of that same sensation would be "sore," "painful," or "pulling."

To illustrate the multiple uses of the word tight, we will use the hamstring muscle as an example. The hamstring is the muscle on the back of your leg, and you stretch it by bending over to touch your toes. Here are some inaccurate reasons it might be called "tight":

1. It's sore. Maybe you just did a workout and you were doing a lot of kettlebell swings, and your hamstring is sore. So when you get up from standing you may grab the back of your hamstring and say, "Oh, my hamstring is so tight." You are using "tight" to describe muscle soreness, an inaccurate definition. Use "sore."

2. You feel a stretching sensation in the back of your leg if you go to bend over to touch your toes and stretch your hamstring. That is a normal sensation that simply lets you know that the muscle is being stretched, not necessarily that the muscle is "tight." Say instead, "I can really feel that stretching!"

3. The back of the leg is being touched and it feels sore. This could be an exercise-induced soreness or an actual injury. "Tight" would be inaccurate. Again, use "sore."

Continuing to use the hamstring as an example, here are more accurate ways to use the word "tight."

4. Let's imagine the same stretch, bending over to touch your toes, where the hands reaching mid-shin is the farthest that can be reached. If the goal for a normal length of the muscle is to allow you to touch the floor and you're falling short, this version of "tight" is describing a lack of motion in a muscle, a muscle that can't quite lengthen fully. This is an accurate definition.

5. The type of "tight" used most in this book is to describe a muscle that has excessive tension or that is "on" when it should be relaxed or "off." We've all experienced that in the upper part of our shoulder with a muscle knot. When a muscle is holding tone, is contracted, is not relaxing, or is knotted it can accurately be called "tight." If you are resting in bed doing nothing and you touch your hamstring and it is hard and contracted or knotted, then it is "tight." It should be relaxed, soft, and supple, but it is not. It's "tight."

You can imagine that when we're using the same term in all these scenarios it can be confusing. I've even had people describe pinching as being "tight." When raising the arm up high and feeling pain on the top of the shoulder, an exclamation of "My shoulder is so tight!" is not accurate. It's actually pinching on tendons in the shoulder! By clarifying how we use "tight," we can better communicate what is happening in the body and better understand the rest of this book.

The most accurate way to use "tight" is to describe a muscle that will not lengthen or a muscle that is holding tension with a knot

The first accurate definition of "tight" is intended to describe the length of the tissue. Let's go back to the hamstring example. When you go down to touch your toes, and you can't reach the floor because your hamstring will not lengthen very much, that would be a good description of a muscle being tight. If you can put your hands completely on the ground when you bend over, but you feel a sensation in the back of your hamstring that's telling you that you're stretching, that's not "tight," that's just stretching. The muscle can lengthen the normal amount that is needed for a healthy functioning body, so that muscle is not tight. It's just being stretched.

The second accurate use of "tight" describes a muscle that's not lengthening very much because the muscle is partially contracted. The muscle has been turned on for some reason by the brain; it's not relaxed. Having a muscle knot or trigger point would be an example of this. When we're not using a muscle it should be nice and soft, supple and relaxed. You should be able to feel it as squishy. If a muscle feels hard when you're not using it, then that muscle is tight. Muscles that are tight because of a knot do not stretch very far, do not contract very well, and cause pain when they are used or stretched. Sometimes they are even painful at rest.

A lot of things happen with muscle knots that we will cover soon, but it's important to be clear moving forward. A "tight" muscle is a muscle that cannot lengthen, either because the muscle fiber won't stretch or the muscle is holding excess tension. Tight does not mean sore, painful, injured, pinching, or stretching.

Knots and Triggers

A muscle knot is a spot inside the muscle itself where some of the muscle fibers are contracted. This section of the muscle stays "on" no matter what you are doing. In fact, these knots can stay contracted for decades without ever relaxing. Knots feel like dense sections in the muscle and often hurt with pressure. A skilled hand can find these knots quite easily as the texture of the tissue feels much different when knotted. Healthy muscle tissue is soft and squishy; knots are dense and hard.

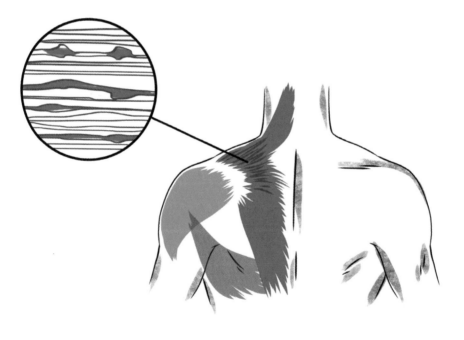

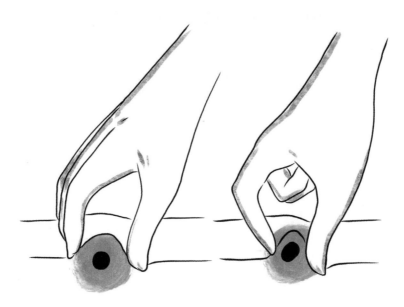

Muscle knots are parts of the muscle that stay contracted

Often, muscle knots will develop as a result of a muscle being used too much, contracted for a long time without relaxation, shortened too long, or in a stressful situation. Muscles are healthiest when they get a break from contracting by turning off often. Too much contracting without relaxing is not a good thing. Once a muscle is "on" for too long or is used too much, the brain decides to keep a part of that muscle contracted for good, creating the knot. It's like the "on" button at the control center gets flipped and the controller goes to lunch. This can happen in a small or large section of the muscle, sometimes even the whole muscle, creating different-sized muscle knots.

In our modern economy of a plethora of computer jobs, muscle knots on the top of the shoulder area (upper trapezius) is common. With the arms reaching out in front of the body all day long, the upper trapezius muscle is constantly "on" to prevent the shoulders from falling forward and to keep your head from rolling off your shoulders. This is happening to me right now as I write this book! After a long day of work, this muscle will likely stay contracted when you're done typing, even when you're walking, sleeping, or eating as the day goes on. The switch is stuck in the "on" position.

Muscle knots also develop in muscles that are in a shortened position for too long. Muscles like to be at their ideal length, not too long (they get weak) and not too short (they get tight and weak). When short, they get cramped and easily develop knots, especially when you ask them to work when they are short. Many of the activities listed in the next section cause muscle knots in the iliacus and psoas because of this reason, being asked to work hard in a shortened position.

Another reason for the development of a muscle knot is stress or emotional trauma. When the brain perceives a threat of some sort, it will contract a muscle or two to protect the area that seems threatened. Even with generalized stress, the neck and shoulders and the hips and pelvis are common areas for muscle tension. The brain wants to protect its home in the skull (neck and shoulder tension protects the head) and our vital organs in the abdomen (hip and pelvis tension protects the organs).

Physical trauma can cause a knot to develop as well. If you sprain your ankle, the muscles around the ankle will protect it by turning on and staying on, creating a knot in efforts to keep the ankle stable. If you have hip surgery, the muscles around the hip might turn on and stay on to protect that traumatized area, creating a knot there. Our brain creates tension wherever it feels the body would benefit from extra protection to increase the survival of the body as long as possible. You can't blame the brain for trying to keep you alive!

When a muscle knot develops, it affects the health and vitality of the muscle itself. A constantly contracted muscle squeezes all the blood vessels that go through it, making it difficult for the blood to flow. It's like stepping on a hose and expecting to easily water the garden. Good blood circulation is vital to the health of the muscle. It's the blood that brings nutrients to the muscle so it can have the energy to have strength and repair itself. This same blood takes away toxins and waste created from muscle contraction. If we don't have good circulation, bringing in new nutrients and cleaning out the gunk, then we end up with a swamp. Some of the gunk that collects in the swamp is calcium and mineral deposits that actually cause the muscle to contract even more. This strengthens the grip of the knot and helps it to stay contracted long-term.

A trigger point is a type of muscle knot with a magical power. When you press on a trigger point, whether it's with your finger or with a tool, that pressure triggers pain in a completely different location than where you are pressing. For example, if you have a knot of the trigger point type in the top of your shoulder and you press on it, it might hurt right where you are pressing, but it could also refer a trigger pain to come up to your head and could give you a headache.

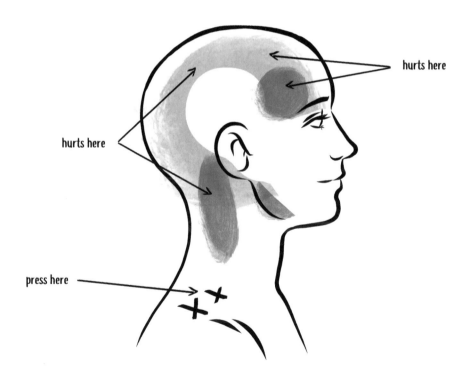

Trigger points are muscle knots that trigger pain somewhere else

Trigger points are important to understand because often we have pain in certain areas in the body that are actually coming from a completely different location. In this example, there is not really something wrong with the head; the problem lies in the muscle on top of the shoulder. It's the top of the shoulder that needs to be treated, not the head.

Trigger points can refer to lots of places. Pain down the arm could result from pressing on the shoulder blade. Pain down the leg could be due to a trigger point on the outside of the hip. There are certain patterns that are consistent from person to person. Travell, Simons, & Simons did a wonderful job cataloging these patterns in *Myofascial Pain and Dysfunction: The Trigger Point Manual*, so we can identify the cause of triggered pain with ease. I've included some of the more common trigger point referral patterns of the hip in the section "Releasing Neighboring Tight Spots."

There are two types of trigger points. Latent trigger points are hidden below the surface—you don't know you have them until they are pressed upon. You feel fine, you don't notice any pain, but then someone presses on that muscle knot in your shoulder and it hurts! Suddenly you're feeling pain all the way up into your head from pressure on your shoulder. It's "latent" because it's not active. It's just below the surface, waiting to trigger pain somewhere else.

If you go to town rubbing a latent trigger point or overusing that muscle, it could quickly activate, becoming an active trigger point. This active trigger point is one which is causing a referral pain without pushing on it. Using the same example, you would have a headache without even touching the trigger point in the shoulder. If you press on that active trigger point in the shoulder, it'll make the headache even more intense.

Our muscles work a lot better when they are not bound in a knot. They can be long, strong, and pain-free when they are released from their tension. Stretching, rubbing, warming, and pressing are different techniques that are used in an attempt to relieve tight muscles. They all work in different ways and to different degrees. It's important to understand how these techniques differ when looking to loosen up that tight hip of yours.

Different ways to address an unhappy muscle: stretch, rub, press

Stretching Isn't Enough

Stretching a muscle makes it longer by moving the body in a specific way to lengthen it. For example, if you're stretching your hamstring and you bend down to touch your toes, that motion makes the hamstring muscle get longer and stretch.

Stretching works by bringing blood flow to the muscle. This is particularly useful when you have a knot or you've been inactive and you want that circulation to come to the area to clean up the toxins and bring some nutrients to the muscles. Stretching warms up the muscles by increasing blood flow and by increasing the pliability of the muscle. Just like when you pull on dough and it goes from being hard to soft, muscles soften when stretched.

The brain gets a special message from a muscle when it is stretched too. There are many different types of nerves in the muscle itself that are sending information to the brain, information about how fast, how hard, and how long the muscle is moving. When the stretch is gentle, the brain gets the hint to release some tension in that muscle because the brain sees this motion as safe and predictable. The brain feeling safe is what allows for more mobility and flexibility in a muscle. Muscles don't actually grow muscle fibers or get longer when they become more flexible. If a muscle stretches more than it has before, it's solely due to the brain feeling comfortable and allowing the muscle to do so.

Stretching also prepares the muscle for movement and it activates the nerves that connect to the muscle to get it ready for action. It also teaches the muscle how to grow new muscle or repair broken muscle in the correct way. If you are building a ladder, you want to line up the rungs so that they are all the same distance apart and parallel to each other; you don't want to nail on the rungs haphazardly. Similarly, when a muscle is repairing, you want the new muscle tissue to line up properly. Stretching teaches the muscle how to do this. If you did injure your hamstring, for example, gently stretching it as it heals allows it to repair properly.

When it comes to muscle knots, stretching can provide some mild relief. The increased circulation and the effect on the brain do allow for the muscle to relax a bit. Often, it is not enough to release a knot completely, but it is an important and effective part of the recovery process.

Rubbing May Make it Worse

Massaging a muscle involves rubbing, manipulating, or moving it. There are many different kinds of massage strokes that can be used, and they increase the circulation to the muscle as well. Massage also affects the brain to help relax the muscles and the body as a whole. We all know that touch is therapeutic and calming. This is why we rub the back of a child who's upset or why we flock to get a massage when stressed. Firm rubbing can also soften the experience of pain as the firm pressure blocks some of the pain signals interpreted by the brain. Massage is also helpful to break up tissue that is unhealthy or scarred so that the body can rebuild itself better. There are even massage techniques that release tension in the fascia that surrounds the muscles that can help the body function at its best.

Self-massage techniques such as foam rollers, sticks, balls, and tools that move and vibrate are prevalent. All of these techniques are moving the muscle around, increasing the circulation, preparing the tissue to heal, and calming the brain's hold on the tension of the body. If the muscle that is being massaged has a latent trigger point in it, however, the manipulation of the muscle will likely activate that trigger point and make the symptoms worse instead of better. This is one reason why many complain of worsening pain after a massage.

These two techniques, stretching and massage, work differently than putting prolonged pressure on the muscle. I make this distinction because a lot of people go in for a massage, use a foam roller, or use some sort of massage tool, hoping to relax their muscle knots. Although stretching and massage can help with muscle knots to some degree, the most effective way to release tension in a muscle knot or a trigger point is simply direct constant pressure.

Warm it up, Buttercup

One way to release the tension in a muscle is through introducing more circulation to the area. Both stretching and massage, as mentioned above, improve circulation. Circulation also increases with exercise, magnets, and heat methods such as a hot pack, sauna, hot tub, bath or shower, ultrasound, and forms of infrared light like a therapeutic laser, a biomat (a mat that gives infrared light), and an infrared sauna. Even being out in the sun helps (one of the many reasons it feels good to be outside). When circulation is increased to the muscle knot in one way or another, some of those mineral deposits and toxins get swept away. This gives that muscle more of a chance to relax. Increasing circulation to the area is a simple tool that works fairly well in addition to other techniques for muscle knots and tension.

Pressure Is the Golden Ticket

Some muscle knots and trigger points can get better just by increasing circulation. For most muscle knots, however, it's not that simple. Using pressure to release the tension is often necessary (Travell, Simons, & Simons). Pressure release (often called trigger point release) is different than massaging the muscle, rolling on a foam roller, vibrating a muscle, releasing the fascia, or stretching. All of these are useful techniques, but they're not nearly as effective at releasing muscle knots and trigger points as prolonged pressure.

Pressure release technique involves finding the dense and contracted area of the tissue and putting prolonged pressure on that particular spot. The prolonged pressure at first will cause pain at the location of the pressure; it will be sore, and that's OK. If it's a trigger point, the pressure will soon cause a referral pain that will go somewhere else. Sometimes that referral pain feels dull, sometimes numb, sometimes intense. Remember the shoulder muscle causing a headache example? Holding constant pressure on the muscle knot will create a quick surge of increased circulation and change the pattern in the brain that is making that muscle stay contracted.

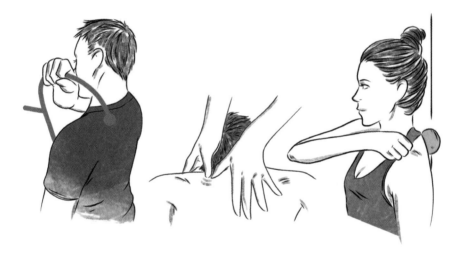

Ways to deliver prolonged pressure

The key to this technique is *prolonged* pressure. You can't just press it for a few seconds and then be done because that can activate a trigger point and will not soften it. You don't want to make it angrier; you want your efforts to produce results! The ticket is finding the knotted spot and holding it, without rubbing or moving, for thirty to ninety seconds, or as long as it takes for the pain that's referring to mostly go away. Maintaining the pressure without moving will allow that trigger point to relax to its optimal soft and supple state.

Up until now, the brain has chosen to hold tension in this muscle for some reason. Prolonged pressure finally tells the brain that it can now allow that muscle to relax. The exhausted, swamp-filled muscle finally is free of its arduous work. No wonder it feels so good! If this pattern of the muscle knot is not treated, it would likely persist indefinitely. We are breaking an unhealthy pattern in the tissue.

Let's reiterate one more time the important distinction between rubbing and stationary pressure. I can't tell you how many clients of mine have left their massage sessions with more pain or headaches as a result of trigger points being activated by rubbing and not deactivated by pressure release. This prolonged pressure method along with warming up the muscle with stretching and heat is how we will release your tight hip.

Happy Muscles Don't Hurt

As a self-mastery exercise, I encourage you to learn what you are supposed to feel in your body when you do specific motions, techniques, exercises, or stretches. If you don't know what you should feel, or you are feeling something different than what you should, you could be hurting yourself. I have seen clients doing a stretch incorrectly for years, even causing damage, because they didn't clearly know what they were supposed to feel. What they were actually feeling was not what was intended for the stretch. This is something to pay close attention to.

If, when performing a stretch to open up the chest muscles, for example, it is felt in between the shoulder blades and not the chest, the benefit of the stretch is lost and the shoulder blades are getting aggravated. Just because you can feel *something* doesn't mean it's the right thing to feel. It is your responsibility to know not only how to do a stretch or exercise, but exactly what you should be feeling. Ask your instructor, coach, or therapist what you are supposed to feel. If you don't feel the exact sensation that you should, then you are either not doing it correctly or the movement is not for you. If you are supposed to feel something specific with a stretch or exercise but you don't, that movement might not be doing anything at all for you; don't waste your time.

39

PART 2:
WHY IS MY HIP SO TIGHT?

Yes, I'm sorry to say, it is true, we all have tight hips. Unfortunately, this phenomenon isn't going away anytime soon. It comes with a modern life full of sitting and stress. The culprit is that iliopsoas muscle. Iliacus and psoas are in a shortened position when we sit and that, over time, makes them tight.

Beyond sitting there are many other reasons why this muscle gets tight. It can be from certain athletic endeavors that overuse that muscle or cause strain to the joints it protects. In a different way, those that are very flexible, especially in the lower back and hips, end up with tight iliopsoas muscles as the body tries to stabilize that which is too mobile. Tightness can also arise because of injuries, internal organ issues, stress, and trauma.

Given such a long list of reasons, there's a really good chance that you, your neighbor, your yoga teacher, and your boss all have some sort of tightness in the hips. This tightness then affects the rest of the body in some way, shape, or form. On a brighter note, there are some simple lifestyle hacks that can soften the effect of this hip-tightening life we live. But first, let's explore these various causes of tightness of iliopsoas in detail.

Sitting Too Long

Most of us sit for more than twelve hours a day, every day, then add in the commute! Even sitting for a couple of hours at a time can cause a tightening of the iliopsoas. Sitting puts the iliopsoas in a shortened position because the distance between the leg and the body is shortened. We learned in the previous section "Knots and Triggers" that a muscle that is in a shortened position for a long period of time gets cramped, becomes swampy, and eventually develops muscle knots.

Sitting shortens and overuses the iliopsoas

The act of sitting also uses the iliacus and the psoas quite a bit, asking those shortened muscles to work the entire time. The iliacus keeps your pelvis stationary relative to your thigh bone, and your psoas helps hold your spine straight in sitting. They hold you up. If you were to completely shut off your iliopsoas, you wouldn't be able to sit upright.

Gravity encourages us to slouch when we are sitting. When we slouch that takes a little bit of that slack off of that muscle and it doesn't have to work so hard. However, even though the iliopsoas gets a little break, the low back and upper body suffer from poor posture, causing a whole host of other issues. So sitting nice and tall is still optimal although it makes that shortened and cramped iliopsoas muscle work overtime. This is why getting up from your desk to give the muscle a break at least every thirty minutes is essential. In "Sitting Tips," this is discussed in detail, but for now, know that sitting all day is a disaster waiting to happen.

After sitting at a desk all day long, the iliopsoas muscle can turn "on" for good because it has been contracting in a short position for too long. Everything you do next is with a knotted iliopsoas: lying down, resting, walking, it's still contracting. Once that muscle turns on, it tends to stay on unless you do something about it.

Driving Too Far

When driving, like sitting, a knot or trigger point can quickly develop in the iliacus or psoas because those muscles are asked to work for a long time in a short position, a recipe for disaster. People typically are very stationary when in a car, not moving around much. Having to reach for the pedals, and leaning partially back, we lose some of the stability we get sitting in a regular chair. In addition, being the driver, you are constantly using the right iliacus and psoas to accelerate and break. The left one gets a little work too if shifting with a manual transmission. The iliopsoas has to be partially contracted to be ready to move from one pedal to the next on a dime. It's really hard to let those muscles relax while you're driving because a good driver is prepared to brake at any time. It's even worse in traffic, going back and forth from acceleration to braking. I can't wait for self-driving cars!

When you're driving for an extended amount of time—on a long road trip, a commute for work, driving the kids to and fro, driving around for your job itself—an overuse of the iliacus and psoas muscles will occur. This naturally increases the chance of developing a tight and unhappy pair. Just sitting and driving is plenty of reason for most people to have tight iliacus and psoas muscles, but other activities can contribute as well.

Driving involves constant use of the iliopsoas in a shortened position

Athletics and Fitness

Athletic and fitness endeavors involve a wide variety of movements, from squatting to kicking, running, lunging, pushing, or quickly changing directions. All of these motions involve the iliopsoas in some way, because it is the muscle group that connects the upper and lower body, and, in all of these activities, we are using both. Certain sports do have a higher incidence of issues with the iliopsoas muscle, but every sport and fitness activity does involve the iliopsoas in some way.

Running

Nearly all runners have a tight iliopsoas. Running utilizes the iliopsoas to swing the leg forward in a running pattern while simultaneously stabilizing the spine and hips. The leg strides forward using the iliopsoas and when the leg extends behind the body, that muscle is stretching. Any time there is one leg forward and another leg behind while using this muscle, there is a good chance for one of the iliopsoas muscles to develop tightness. Additionally, this cycle of repetitive contraction and stretch combined with the role of stabilizing the spine and hips easily fatigues and overuses the muscles, further encouraging a state of tightness. In my experience, many runners with tight iliopsoas muscles have resolved their pain in other parts of the body such as the glute, knee, foot, and toe, by releasing this tension.

Running overuses the iliopsoas

Lunging

Lunging is involved in many sports such as tennis, soccer, basketball, and baseball. During a lunging motion, there is a high risk of irritating the iliopsoas for the same reason as running, asking the muscle to move the leg forward while the other is behind the body, an unstable position, all while asking the muscle to also stabilize. The leg that's going forward in the lunge is utilizing the iliopsoas on that side and puts that muscle in a shortened position, working while it's short. At the same time, the iliopsoas that is on the back leg in the lunge is being stretched. When there's a quick lunge motion where the body is a bit unstable, going for a ball on the basketball court, for example, and the body or the brain may not be quite ready for it, the brain might tell the iliopsoas to tighten up to protect the area. You could be playing tennis for twenty years with no issues and then one day you go to lunge for a ball and the muscle gets scared and tightens up.

Lunging makes the iliopsoas have to work hard to stabilize the
hip in an unpredictable situation

Sharon recently came into my office enthusiastic to get her glute released. She had previously received temporary relief from massages to her glute area, and she heard I had magic hands. Her hope was that I could give her an even better massage to get that muscle to stop hurting her for good. She demonstrated the four glute stretches she diligently performed daily and shared with me her weekly massage routine. She had been having a pain in the butt for the last few years, ever since she had lunged for a ball on the tennis court that one day.

She loved her massage therapist and how she would "get in there" to loosen up her glute. The stubborn nature of that glute would consistently present itself, compelling her massage therapist to say, "Wow, that glute is so tight. We need to keep chipping away at it." Years had passed and her love for her massage sessions had grown, feeling great as she left each session. Except the pain kept coming back. "Maybe I just need to stretch more," she thought. At this point, she thought she would have to live with this pain for the rest of her life. She had actually stopped playing tennis for a year and took up other activities that didn't stress this area the same way.

Standing in my office, I could see that her right hip was rotated forward, the same side where she was having the pain in her glute. This was confirmed when she laid down and the right leg looked long but then got short when she sat up, indicating a right anteriorly rotated pelvis. Placing my hands on the inside surface of the pelvic bone, where the iliacus muscle lives, I could feel that the right side was dense and the left side was soft.

We spent fifteen minutes together. I placed precise and prolonged pressure on the right iliacus with my fingertips. The muscle melted from thick to juicy during this short period of time. I applied a hot laser to the area for some deep heat and taught her a couple of exercises (that you'll learn soon) to help realign her pelvis and to keep those muscles relaxed.

A few hours later, the phone rang. With awe she reported that this was the first time in two years that her glute pain wasn't bothering her at all. That relief continues to this day. She remarked that we didn't even touch her glute and it still got better.

Sharon is a classic example of experiencing a quick lunging position that is unexpected or particularly challenging causing that iliopsoas muscle to get too challenged, tightening up as a result. The iliopsoas acted like a watchdog, and the constant tightness created a tug-of-war with the piriformis and glute muscles (the Villains), making them tight too. The glute tension was never going to go away with massage unless the cause of the problem was addressed. That cause was the tight iliacus.

Bicycling

Riding a bicycle involves a compressed position that is bent at the hip, putting the iliopsoas in a shortened and cramped position. Remember, muscles don't like to work when they are short. Using clips on the pedals improperly by pulling up further activates the already cramped iliopsoas. The repetitive nature of bicycling and having that muscle in its shortened position, without standing up and lengthening back out again, makes developing a tight iliopsoas quite common for bikers. Once the muscle gets tightened it could stay on for good, affecting you throughout the day in ways you are not aware.

Bicycling shortens the iliopsoas and makes it work extra hard

Kicking

Martial arts, kickboxing, soccer, and football are some examples of kicking sports. When kicking the leg forward, the iliopsoas works very hard to move that leg forward while stabilizing the spine and hip. One leg swinging backward and forward while the other is stable creates that challenging situation of asking the muscle to produce force and hold the area together at the same time. Repetitive kicking creates a tendency for the iliopsoas to get overused as well. Kicking in an unpredictable situation, maybe a kick that is unexpectedly blocked, for example, can also cause that muscle to react by being tight as a protective mechanism. The threatening situation can send a signal to your brain that something happened that wasn't quite expected and that can cause tightness of the iliopsoas. All of this creates a prime opportunity for that muscle to decide to stay on and knot up. It can forget how to turn off and stay tight until you teach it how to relax again.

Kicking requires a lot of force from the iliopsoas while it's also asked to stabilize the core

Heavy Lifting

The primary role of the iliacus and the psoas muscle is to stabilize the connection of the lower back to the pelvis and hips. Stabilizing means holding everything together, keeping the joints from moving in ways that can cause injury. Heavy lifting involves having the lower back, hips, and pelvis stable while squatting or lifting something. The amount of weight that is lifted increasingly puts more and more strain on those stabilizing muscles. They have to work extra hard to keep the midsection held together. When the iliopsoas muscles are working too hard to do this stabilizing job, they can get scared and decide to stay contracted for good. At some point in a weight lifting regimen, it's likely that these muscles will get overworked and want to stay tight.

Heavy lifting requires the iliopsoas to work overtime
to stabilize the core

There are some really great benefits to doing deep squats where the butt gets close to the heels. The ability to train this way does improve athletic performance, especially explosiveness. The iliopsoas, unfortunately, is in a really shortened position with a deep squat, so although it's improving explosiveness, it is also increasing the risk of developing tightness in that muscle. Asking a muscle to work in a shortened position is a tall order. Muscles function better in their mid-range of motion. Combining the shortened position of the iliopsoas in a deep squat with the hard work it has in store keeping that area of the body stable, while handling heavy weights, creates a prime opportunity for tightness to develop that won't go away when you stop.

Imbalances in Strength and Flexibility

When one area of the body is much stronger than an opposite area of the body it creates imbalance. Just ask a baseball pitcher or a tennis player how one-sided activities affect their body. Ultimately, our bodies work the best when they are in balance. A perfect example of an imbalance is with the bench press. When the front of the body, the chest muscles, get really strong without strengthening the back of the body, the muscles in between the shoulder blades end up getting weaker and strained. The stronger chest muscles then pull the shoulders forward, straining the neck and shoulders as a result.

Following this logic, the iliopsoas can become tight because of weakness in the muscles on the outside and back of the hip. Because these work opposite of each other, if there is very little strength in the back of the hip and the iliopsoas muscles are really strong in the front, this imbalance will let the iliopsoas win and be tight. Another example would be imbalances in flexibility. If you were working really hard on the flexibility of your hamstring on the back of the leg but you weren't working at all on the front, the tightness in your quadricep and iliopsoas will win. They will be pulling you forward and will tend to tighten up even more. It's a basic game of tug-of-war.

Strength and flexibility imbalances can involve lots of different components as the body is quite complex. Working with a personal trainer, physical therapist, or other professional can help you identify those imbalances and help you figure out how to inch towards balance. Imbalance in strength and flexibility around the spine and hips, such as weak glutes, loose hamstrings, or tight quads, can cause a tight iliacus.

Hips Too Open

Many very flexible folks, such as yogis, dancers, and gymnasts, surprisingly have really tight iliopsoas muscles. They may be able to go very deep into a hip flexor stretch and not feel much at all, but laying down, their iliacus and their psoas muscles are indeed tight, showing up as knots in the muscle. This pattern is predictable. They would pass all the standard physical therapy tests for the length of the iliopsoas, appearing to be flexible in this muscle. After many years of improving flexibility, they may be able to bring their legs up behind their head, do the splits, and all sorts of contortions. But at rest, those muscles are unexpectedly holding tension. If this tension is present even when they are completely lying down and not lifting a finger, it is there all day long.

People who are hypermobile and are taking their bodies through an extreme range of motion are really challenging the iliacus and psoas muscles. Remember, it's the job of the iliopsoas to stabilize and hold it all together. A very flexible body has loose joints to contend with and therefore, extra work is required of the iliopsoas to hold the joints together. Furthermore, when the hip is asked to go into one of those unstable positions in yoga, dance, or gymnastics, the iliopsoas can easily decide to turn the switch to "on" for good in attempts to hold everything together.

Yoga, Gymnastics, Dance

Hypermobility is encouraged in yoga, dance, and gymnastics. Those who are naturally flexible have positive reinforcement as they watch themselves excel in comparison to their peers. Most that are drawn to yoga, dance, and gymnastics need more stability than flexibility to be in balance but, because they are such naturals, they end up stretching more and more, making the body have to work even harder to keep it stabilized.

Hips can become too flexible in yoga, gymnastics, and dance, making the iliopsoas have to work even harder to stabilize that area

The term "hip openers" has become such a popular term used in the yoga community as a core part of a desirable healthy yoga body. The reality is that hips are meant to have a basic level of range of motion, but they are meant to be strong and stable, not "open." Unfortunately, the focus on this end goal of "open hips" is detrimental, creating hips that are too open.

The job of the hip and the pelvis is to connect these legs that are moving us around this planet with the spine that is keeping us upright. This is why the muscles around this area are so huge—they have to move us *and* keep us stable. If we don't have stability then things start to fall apart, shift around, and wear down.

This whole idea of opening up the hips and creating more space in the hips *is* an idea that is useful for people who have very tight hips. Some of us tend to be really stiff and tight and need more flexibility, and yoga is a great form of exercise for those kinds of bodies. In contrast, those who are already really mobile and can easily get into a deep lunge or fold forward with their hands to the ground already have a very flexible hip and do not need their hips opened more.

People who are dancers, gymnasts, and yogis tend to work on postures like the splits, a deep pigeon pose, a flatter forward fold, getting the legs behind the head, or kicking the legs up to the nose. All of these extreme motions bring the lower back, hips, and pelvis into positions that are outside of what these joints are really designed to do. As a result, the iliacus and the psoas muscle will tend to tighten up to protect that area and try to hold everything together. This type of tightness is deceiving because the muscle is holding tension even though the athlete can move their body in all kinds of ways, giving the illusion that they are not tight one bit.

I know this is true from personal experience. Genetically, I have a lot of mobility in my body, and so do my children. I was really excited to start yoga and was easily satisfied when I could do many of the poses in yoga quite easily. After practicing for about five years, and getting deeper into the poses, listening to my body and progressing gently, I continued to excitedly progress into deeper poses. Unfortunately, the more my yoga practice progressed the tighter my iliopsoas would be afterward. It got to the point where I would have a tight hip when I was sitting and I couldn't get comfortable while sleeping, even though I was doing my daily yoga practice that I thought was good for me. I started using a ball to help release my iliopsoas before and after my yoga practice, but it wasn't until I stopped stretching so deeply that the tightness resolved.

Yoga, dance, and gymnastics also involves many motions that isolate and overwork the hip flexor muscles as well. Yoga poses such as staff pose, boat pose, and standing hand to toe rely heavily on the iliopsoas for strength, and a pose like child's pose puts the iliopsoas in a cramped position. The splits and kicks in dance and gymnastics are iliopsoas-dominant poses too. These are examples of activities that can aggravate an already unhappy muscle, maybe even push it over the edge into a knot.

My daughter, Autumn, who is naturally flexible and encouraged to keep stretching deeper

Finally getting to the level of dancing on the high school dance team is thrilling. With practices nearly every day full of kicks, leaps, and turns, Molly was ignoring her constant back pain. It worsened towards the end of each practice and even bothered her at school. How could a young and active sophomore in high school have back pain? Upon discovery that her pelvis on her painful side was rotated forward because her iliopsoas on that side was tight, we went to work. While completely resting on the treatment table, the iliacus wasn't relaxed when it had absolutely no work to do. Tenderness and a knotted muscle presented itself on the opposite glute area too, as did tenderness at the joint where the tailbone and pelvis connect (the sacroiliac joint).

By releasing the tension in the iliacus muscle in the front of her hip and the tension on the opposite glute with my magic hands, the pain started to loosen its grip. Wide-eyed, she got off the table the very first visit and remarked that, for the first time in years, her back pain was gone. With a few stretches and the pelvic realignment exercise (part of the "3 Simple Steps" to follow) she was well on her way to recovery. Within a month's time, her pain had completely gone away. She didn't really need the taping techniques I taught her or the last few PT sessions we had scheduled because her pain resolved with the release of that iliacus muscle. As a person who had been dealing with pain for so long, she was thrilled. If she would have only known about her iliacus muscle and what to do to keep it healthy, she could have resolved it on her own in no time.

Bone Shapes

All of us have different shapes of the ball and socket of our hip. Yoga instructor Paul Grilley (paulgrilley.com) teaches on this topic of bony difference when it comes to yoga and helps practitioners set realistic expectations of their bodies during their practice. Take a look at the illustration below: two different pelvic bones side by side. The one that's to the left has a much deeper socket; the one on the right has a much shallower socket. The shallower the socket, the more mobility the hip has, and if it's too shallow, the hip can become unstable, making the iliopsoas have to work hard to hold it together. You can also see how the left pelvis has sockets facing more forward, and the pelvis on the right has sockets facing more to the side. The angle of the ball of the thigh bone in relation to the shaft of the bone can also vary widely. These differences determine whether one can cross their legs easily and really impacts what motions are physically possible. Trying to push beyond what your unique bones will allow sets the stage for joint issues and frustration.

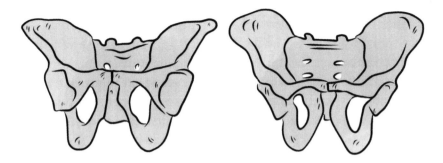

Each person's pelvic and thigh bones are shaped differently. Look at the difference in just the hip socket in this example.

Your unique bone shape is an important consideration when it comes to whether you have a tendency towards having a tight iliopsoas. Because one of the primary jobs of the iliacus is to affect the orientation of the pelvic bone to make sure the socket is at the right angle for the ball to fit, the health of the iliacus is crucial in cases where a good fit of the ball into the socket is a challenge. If your socket is shallow, you may have hip dysplasia, a ball that doesn't fit well in the socket. In this situation there is not a lot of stability in the hip and the iliacus has to work harder, easily creating a situation where the muscle turns "on" for good. Alternatively, if you have a really deep socket and the ball fits in there nicely, you have a lot more stability and the iliacus doesn't have to work so hard to keep you stable.

With the wide variety of possible bone structures, you can see the possibility for an unstable hip exists regardless of whether you do excessive stretching or not. Your bone structure has a lot to do with what shape your body takes when doing various motions. When trying to follow a technique for a particular stretch or exercise, this is important to know. If it doesn't feel right, modify for your bone type. Seek help from someone who can help you understand your anatomy and how that impacts how *your* particular body moves.

Merry had a nagging thigh pain that brought her to an orthopedic surgeon in hopes of a cure. Years had passed with no reprieve from this pain that started during a hot yoga class and never went away.

Her X-rays showed a shallow hip socket (hip dysplasia), and a hip replacement was casually offered to her by the doctor.

At thirty-seven, Merry was skeptical of a surgery so drastic; she ended up seeking physical therapy in desperation. It was discovered that her iliacus was awfully tight on the side of her thigh pain. Having an unstable hip and doing deep yoga poses in a hot room where the muscles and joints were way too loosey-goosey presented a prime opportunity for the iliacus to switch into high gear, turn on, and protect that joint.

Placing prolonged pressure on her iliacus near her pelvis, the pain way down in her thigh intensified, indicating the presence of a trigger point in her iliacus as the cause of her persistent thigh pain. Her face spelled amazement as that confident smile of mine met hers. After a minute or two of holding that pressure point, the thigh pain started to fade for the first time in years. With modifications to her yoga practice and a focus on strength instead of flexibility, she had months of no pain at all. Because she was born with a shallow hip socket, she needs to have her iliacus released from time to time because with normal daily activities, that muscle does have to work harder than most to keep the hip joint stable, sometimes creating a trigger point as a result. She uses the Hip Hook (coming up in "3 Simple Steps") to release the iliacus tension herself, as needed, avoiding surgery and pain.

Loosey-Goosey

Excess mobility can also be acquired from certain disease processes and medications. Some of us are hypermobile at birth due to genetic causes. These genetic causes make the connective tissue that holds everything together stretchier and less stable. Connective tissue is made up of elastin, which is stretchy, and collagen, which is stiff. Based on genetics and age, the ratio of elastin to collagen differs; everyone is different. The more collagen in the connective tissue, the more strength it has to better hold the joints together. The more elastin in the connective tissue, the stretchier and looser the joints become. Whether it's acquired over time or a genetic predisposition to being hypermobile, a loose body sets the stage for tight muscles as the muscles have to hold you together because the bones and connective tissue are not. In the hip region, this could mean a tight iliacus. Those with hypermobility syndrome need less stretching and more strengthening exercises as part of their routine.

If you can create these positions with your hand and elbow, you may have genetic or acquired hypermobility. These figures are taken from the Beighton scale—a tool used by professionals to determine hypermobility syndrome

Pregnancy

Pregnancy releases a chemical in your body called relaxin. This particular hormone is responsible for softening and relaxing some of the connective tissue around the pelvis so that when you're ready to give birth, the baby can smoothly come out of the birth canal. Because this hormone loosens the ligaments that hold the hip and pelvis together, these joints become lax during and after pregnancy. This explains why a lot of women who are pregnant end up with back, tailbone, or hip pain. As I'm sure you can see by now, this instability causes the muscles around the pelvis to tighten excessively, leading to tailbone, back, and hip pain.

Pregnancy and various birthing positions can strain
the pelvis and the iliopsoas muscle

During the delivery process, the position of the baby and the birthing position can also put the iliopsoas into a shortened or strained position. Because the pelvis is already hypermobile, that iliopsoas is working really hard to keep it together, and certain delivery positions stretch the unstable pelvis more or put the iliopsoas in a shortened and easy to tighten position. It's very common, not only during pregnancy but also after pregnancy, to have issues with a tight iliopsoas that doesn't want to relax.

Injuries and Pain

Any time you have some sort of trauma to the body, maybe a strain, surgery, or pain, the body sees this as a threat. It is the brain's responsibility to keep us safe, so the brain's natural directive is to tell muscles around the traumatized area to contract to keep us from harm. If you don't move the area, the brain reasons, it will be safe. For example, if you go to pick up something too heavy and you strain your back, your back muscles will be painful and contract and spasm because they don't want you to move again and hurt yourself. It's amazing how effective pain and muscle tightness is in keeping us from moving! With injuries, this tightening is necessary to prevent you from moving so that area can heal. It's just the brain's way of trying to keep you safe.

Hip Arthritis

Hip arthritis that is inflamed is a major cause of tightness in the iliopsoas muscles. As we mentioned before, the iliacus and psoas attach very close to the hip joint itself. Those muscles are laying right on top of the joint and it's very common for those muscles to tighten to try to stabilize and protect the injured joint and keep you from moving. If you have hip arthritis that is bothering you, your instinct is to not move much because there is pain. The joint actually needs the opposite—it needs to move and have balanced strength around the joint instead.

Hip Labrum

Similar to hip arthritis, if you have a torn or strained hip labrum (a specialized cartilage in the hip joint), you may also have a tight iliacus. Irritation to the hip joint, like a torn labrum, similarly tightens the iliopsoas to protect the hip joint. Some of the symptoms associated with a hip labrum issue are similar to what happens when you have a tight iliopsoas, further emphasizing the role of this muscle in this condition. (See more on arthritis and the labrum in Part 3 under "... Hip Joint")

Low Back or Tailbone Pain

If you have lower back, tailbone, or SI (sacroiliac) joint pain, there's a good chance that you're going to have issues with a tight iliopsoas. The psoas attaches to the spine, and the iliacus attaches to the inside of the pelvis. Those are both responsible for the alignment of the lower back and the SI joint. When there is irritation of any of those structures, the body will protect that area by tightening those muscles. For example, if there is an issue with a disc in your lower back, your body will want to keep you from moving to prevent further damage and pain, tightening the iliopsoas. It will rise to the occasion to serve its role and keep you from moving and hurting. If your SI joint is irritated, the iliacus is sure to be involved. This, again, is a chicken or egg scenario. The tightness in the iliopsoas could actually be the cause of your lower back pain or tailbone problem.

Pelvic Pain

Issues related to the pelvic floor and tightness in your iliopsoas often show up together. The iliacus muscle lies right on the inside surface of the pelvic bone and it's intimately connected with the rest of the pelvic floor's inhabitants and muscles. Because the primary job of the iliacus is to stabilize and protect the hip and pelvis, when there are issues with the pelvic floor it's very common for this muscle to get tight to help protect that area. Again, this is one of those "what's the cause and what's the effect?" puzzles. It's very possible the tightness in the iliopsoas is what's actually contributing to the pelvic pain.

Dr. Henry Manor joyfully practiced dentistry for twenty-five years but was on the brink of retirement because he couldn't figure out his pelvic floor pain that was located right between his testicals and anus. He knew it was probably related to his position all day long, sitting in a chair and twisting to the left to work in the mouths of his clients. He was having a lot of pain. His office manager worked endlessly to research and purchase different chairs, only to end up moving them into the crowded storage room. He took more breaks to stand up and relieve the pain but overall, he was not improving. Maybe he would have to sell the practice, or take an early retirement.

Henry's hesitancy to talk about his pelvic floor was palpable, and my enthusiasm to talk about it made it worse for him. Upon a quick look, I noticed the muscles around his hips and pelvis were tight, very tight.

The iliacus stood out as the most severe. It turns out that his tight iliacus was pulling on his pelvic floor, making the muscles and nerves in his pelvic floor unhappy. After prolonged pressure to the iliacus muscle, and giving him a couple of exercises to work on at home, his pelvic pain went away and he no longer needed my help…or a career counselor.

Back, Hip, Knee, Foot Surgery

Surgery is a huge threat to the body. You're getting cut up, for gosh sakes! We already know how threats to the body can cause tightness. It's stressful to have any kind of surgery to begin with. Furthermore, any surgery that involves the spine and lower body (lower back, tailbone, pelvis, hip, knee, foot, or ankle) involves forces through the hip and pelvis, also affecting the iliopsoas muscle. Then, during recovery from the surgery, the body is placed into stationary positions, walking is altered and challenging, and pain is present. All of these scenarios cause the body to want to protect the area and thus tighten that iliopsoas.

Organ Issues

The proximity of the iliopsoas to the digestive, reproductive, and urinary systems gives the muscle a prime opportunity to protect the area by tightening when one of these systems is struggling. For example, if you're having irritable bowel syndrome or any issue with the intestine, for that matter, your body's natural tendency will protect that struggling area by keeping the iliopsoas muscle tight.

The closer the structure is to the muscle the more likely the muscle is involved. The next-door neighbors hear the house alarm go off first, then the store clerk down the street. If there is an issue related to digestion in the ascending part of the large intestine or the ileocecal valve (the valve between the small and large intestine), it's very common to see the right side of the iliacus tighten. Similarly, if there's an issue with the descending colon it's common to see the left iliacus knot up.

Mohammed had recovered well from surgery for an inguinal hernia (a weakening of the abdominal wall that can affect the bowel) a few years ago. His pain had gotten mostly better and the surgery was considered a success. His main complaint when he came to see me was groin pain, and pinching in his hip joint occurred with a simple knee to chest motion. While treating him I used the prolonged pressure technique on the tight iliacus. I soon found as I started pressing on the iliacus that he felt the same symptom that he was having that really brought him to the doctor in the first place for his hernia. This symptom that he thought was related to the hernia was actually a trigger point in the iliacus. Although the surgery was still necessary to repair the hernia, the doctor didn't evaluate the possibility that a trigger point in the iliacus could be what was causing the original pain. Once we relaxed the tension in that muscle, Mohammed's pain went away.

The ovaries are also very close to the iliopsoas muscle, so when they're inflamed for some reason, the body contracts that muscle to keep the area protected. Tightness in this muscle is important to consider because symptoms, such as groin or abdominal pain attributed to an organ, could be coming directly from the iliopsoas muscle and not the organ itself, or vice versa.

Surgery to the abdominal area involves the abdominal wall and the pelvis, whether it's a small arthroscopic or a large incision. A lot of the structures that are typically repaired or removed as a result of abdominal surgery are really close to the iliopsoas muscles. Destruction and repair to that area are perceived by the brain as a threat, resulting in that muscle stepping up to the plate to protect. Also, when there is an incision that cuts through the abdominal muscles, like a C-section scar, that can significantly impact the function of the core muscles, making iliopsoas have to work even more with less help from the abdominal muscles.

Jennifer's hysterectomy was long overdue, and she was back home being waited on by her surprisingly helpful children. She was experiencing a lot of pain nowhere near her incision. She couldn't even rest and it hurt to lie down, even though that was the doctor's orders. Calls to the surgeon's nurse only offered a timid reassurance that pain was normal after surgery. Jennifer logically expected pain in her incisions but not in the back of her leg, but the nurse wasn't worried. "Just take the pain meds we gave you," she recommended.

A quick drive down the block for this post-surgical house call, and lo and behold, the first thing I noticed was her tight iliacus muscle. That stinker of a muscle was pulling her pelvic bone forward, making one of the Villain muscles, the piriformis, tight. This tight piriformis was pressing on her sciatic nerve, causing pain down her leg. We had two sessions of the prolonged pressure technique to release the tension in the iliacus, and she started working on the pelvic realignment exercise and stretching her piriformis muscle. In two days the nerve pain down her leg went away. Jennifer had never had an issue like this before surgery, so it was clear that the positioning of surgery or the threat to that area of the body had activated her body's protective instinct, tightening the iliacus muscle, which played tug-of-war with the piriformis muscle, ultimately causing sciatic pain.

Emotions

Science continues to uncover the role the brain takes in pain and muscle tightness. When the brain perceives an environment or a situation that seems threatening, it will cause pain or tightness in an attempt to keep you safe from harm. The brain will make you feel pain so that you will slow down, retreat, and keep yourself in a cautious state. The brain will also create tension in various places in the body to keep you from moving too much and to protect you. Both pain and tightness are created by the brain to keep you from doing something dangerous.

We all experience stress in different ways, but what we do have in common is that we all have quite a lot of it. Stress shows up in work, family life, relationships, and unexpected circumstances. With these stressors comes tension in the body. A stressful situation, whether it's related to the hip area or not, could contribute to tension in the iliopsoas.

Where the tension will arise varies from person to person, but we commonly hold stress-related tension in either the neck or the hip area. It's not a big mystery why the body would choose to hold tension around the hips and the neck. All of the essential organs lay right next to the iliacus muscle in the pelvis, making it a pretty important area to protect in a threatening situation. Remember the stage packed full with the digestive, urinary, and reproductive systems, along with our major lymph, nerves, and blood vessels. Similarly, the neck is a common area for stress-related tension because it's protecting the brain, the mastermind that controls it all.

If the brain perceives danger, it will create pain and tension as a way of protecting the body. As you can imagine, the more pieces of data from the environment, thoughts, and past experiences that are threatening, the more likely pain and tension will result. It's no wonder that we get tense in a stressful work meeting, when late to pick up your children, and we don't get enough sleep!

Traumatic experiences, by definition, are scary and unpredictable and tend to make their mark in our memories. The pelvic area not only experiences physical and sexual trauma, but due to its location close to the reproductive system, it's a common place for holding tension related to relationships and our sense of survival and safety. When these aspects of our lives are threatened in some way, it is therefore very common for the iliopsoas muscles to contract and protect this area. Trauma affects the brain's sense of safety and can keep a muscle tight for years.

PART 3:
A TIGHT HIP TWISTS
THE CORE

In the previous section, "Why Is My Hip So Tight?" we described many reasons for the iliacus and psoas to tighten. It's likely that more than one of those reasons applies to you. There's plenty of reasons to choose from. Take your pick!

What matters most isn't that you have a tight muscle, however, but how it is affecting you. Maybe your feet hurt from running or your toe has turned into a swollen bunion. Maybe you can't sit for dinner with your family because your pelvic floor or hip hurts too much. The knee or hip arthritis might be getting worse and worse, making you turn to surgery in desperation. We all have our spots that hurt and our motivations for fixing them.

In this next section, we'll be diving into many of the ways that a tight iliacus and psoas muscle can affect the body from head to toe. You will find which part of *your* body is the weakest link on the chain, so you can clearly see what is the cause and what is the symptom. Remember, you need to know the "why" in order to fix the problem for good.

Our body is all connected, head to toe, just like in the song "Dem Bones": "The backbone's connected to the hip bone, the hip bone's connected to the thigh bone, the thigh bone's connected to the knee bone, the knee bone's connected to the shin bone..." This song is not a gimmick. It actually explains, with a good degree of accuracy, how tightness in the hip can cause issues in many other places of the body.

By understanding how various issues in the body can be traced back to iliacus and psoas tightness, we can clearly understand how releasing this tightness in the hip really gets at the source of the problem. This can help resolve issues that are just not getting better otherwise.

The Hip Bone's Connected to the...

A tight iliacus creates a train wreck where one car gets off the track, resulting in a pileup of connected train cars to spill out of line, straining what is holding them together. When the iliacus muscle is holding tension, contracted, or knotted, it pulls the pelvic bone forward relative to the other pelvic bone and tailbone. This is called an anterior rotated pelvis. The position of the pelvic bone is named based on how one of the pelvic bones is positioned relative to the tailbone and the other pelvic bone. For example, a right anteriorly rotated pelvis means that the right pelvic bone is rotated forward relative to the left side.

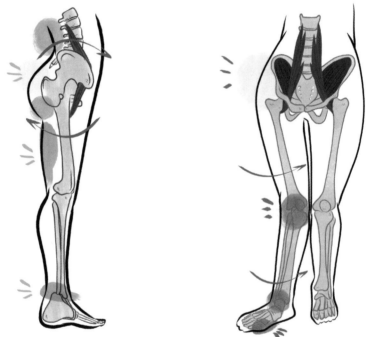

A tight iliacus rotates the pelvis forward and can
cause pain all the way down the chain

The anterior rotation of the pelvis due to a tight iliacus muscle is where the train wreck begins. That tug of the pelvic bone forward relative to the tailbone strains the connection of the pelvis to the tailbone and creates pain and tension where those two bones meet. That junction, the SI (sacroiliac) joint, gets twisted and irritated, and becomes painful.

The first junction of train cars to be affected is the hip joint where the pelvis and thigh bone attach to each other. The hip socket (acetabulum) is supposed to be in a certain position so that the ball of the thigh bone (femur) can fit in perfectly. Because this socket is part of the pelvic bone, and the pelvic bone gets rotated forward when the iliacus muscle is tight, the thigh bone doesn't fit into the socket as intended—the socket is out of place. This rubs the hip joint the wrong way.

This poor fit also causes the thigh bone to rotate inward (internal rotation), affecting the way that the leg works from the hip down. This inward rotation of the thigh bone puts strain on the knee itself and the kneecap doesn't track properly. The next train car, the lower leg, also rotates inward, causing the foot to flatten more (pronate), ultimately affecting the way that the foot and toe is aligned.

The psoas, with its attachment to the front of the thigh bone and to the spine at the lower back, will have the same chain reaction down the leg and up the spine, but the majority of its effect will be on the spine itself. A tight psoas will pull the spine into more of an arch (extension), compressing and side-bending the side of the spine that is tight. All that tugging on the spine irritates all of the structures that live in the lower back, one of the most common locations of pain in the body. The psoas pulling on the spine and the iliacus rotating the pelvis result in a train wreck making its way up the spine to the shoulders, neck, and head as well.

In this next section, each part of the body that can be affected by a tight iliopsoas will be explored. Learning what happens as the effect of a tight iliacus makes its way along the train will give you further clarity for why *you* may need to address your tight iliacus in order to resolve your pain. Feel free to skip to the section that applies to your symptoms, or read through the section entirely to get the full picture.

...Lower Back

The psoas attaches directly to the spine and the iliacus directly to the pelvis, so it is no mystery that tightness in the iliopsoas affects the lower back. The intimate connection of the psoas to the lower back area and its primary job of stabilizing this area make it a common culprit for lower back symptoms. This muscle should be assessed with any issue that arises in this area.

- Facet joint pain
- Disc issues
- Nerve pain
- Back muscle issues
- Scoliosis

When the psoas is tight, it compresses the spine, pulling the spine to the side of its tension, and the tight iliacus rotates that side of the pelvis forward. These motions can cause pinching in the facet joints, the tiny little joints that connect one vertebra to the next. The side that is the tightest will side-bend, twist, and compress the spine, irritating the facet joints, discs, and nerves leaving the spine for the body. When nerves get pinched it can be painful at the spine or anywhere along where that nerve travels. It's not funny to be pinched. When the alignment of the spine is off, it's very common for the muscles that are around the spine to get irritated. There are quite a few muscles in the lower back just waiting to be tight, resulting in muscle tension, strains, and pains in the lower back.

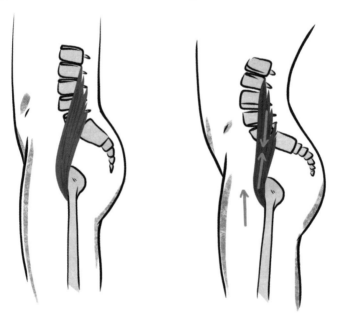

A tight psoas causes a pull on the spine, making the lower back arched, strained, and compressed

One tight psoas pulling harder than the other can be the start of scoliosis. The side-bending and rotational twist of the spine is exactly what happens when there is a tight psoas or iliacus. Already developed scoliosis perpetuates that one-sided tightness, making tight psoas and iliacus muscles quite standard with this condition.

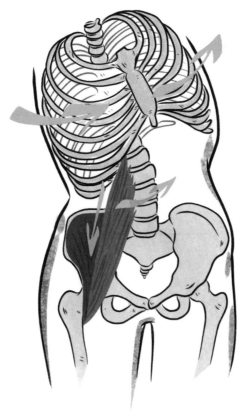

A tight iliopsoas contributing to scoliosis and
rotation of the ribs

...Pelvis

The iliacus attaches to a large area on the inside surface of the pelvis. Its position with its connective tissue blending with all the other structures in the area make it ripe for contributing to pelvic issues. As we know that tissues don't like to be tugged upon, a tight iliacus can be annoying to its neighbors.

- Sacroiliac (SI) joint pain
- Pelvic pain
- Bowel, bladder, and reproductive issues

The tight iliacus pulls the pelvic bone forward, creating strain where the tailbone and the pelvic bone meet. This junction is called the SI (sacroiliac) joint. There are many ligaments and muscles around the SI joint to keep that area stable, and these structures become angry when strained. The piriformis muscle, which is intimate with the sciatic nerve, is one of those muscles that gets tight and inflamed.

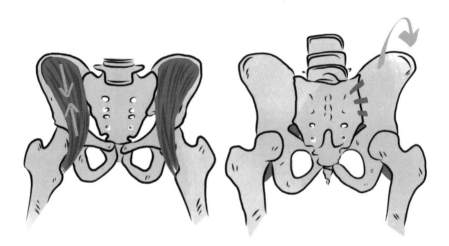

A tight iliacus on one side causes an anterior
rotation and SI pain

Some of the deep hip muscles near the SI joint that get tight and angry as a result of the rotated pelvis and tight iliacus blend with the pelvic floor muscles. The connective tissue of iliacus itself also blends with the bowl of the pelvic floor. This connection translates into pelvic floor tightness and pain when the pelvis is out of alignment and the iliacus is tight. This is due to strain on the pelvic floor muscles, associated muscle tension in those muscles, and nerve irritation in that area.

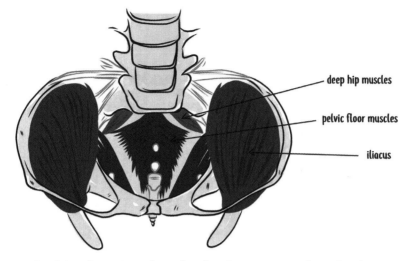

deep hip muscles

pelvic floor muscles

iliacus

Looking down into the pelvic bowl, you can see how the iliacus blends with the pelvic floor

Because the pelvis is the gateway for the bladder, bowel, and reproductive systems, issues with the iliacus and the pelvic floor can affect the function of these systems as well. That rotation of the pelvis can affect the nerves and the muscles that are involved in the health of these systems, resulting in difficulty in this area.

...Hip Joint

This is one of my favorite topics to discuss; there's so much that happens to the hip joint with a tight iliopsoas. Remember how close the iliacus and the psoas attach to the hip joint? They are literally pressed up against it, having quite an effect on the hip.

Rubbing the Wrong Way:

- Hip arthritis

- Hip labrum issues
- Groin pain

Tight All Over:

- Psoas tightness
- Hip flexor tendonitis
- Iliopsoas release surgery
- Glute pain (piriformis, deep rotators, obturator internus)
- Hip bursitis
- Adductor muscle issues

Making a Move:

- Pain getting up from sitting
- Pain with marching
- Pinch with bringing knee to chest
- Hip pop when lowering the leg
- Snapping hip

Rubbing the Wrong Way

When the tires are not aligned and balanced in a car, the tread wears unevenly. Then the tires need to be replaced sooner than you hoped. Similarly, when the tight iliacus pulls the pelvis forward, changing the position of the hip socket, it affects how the ball of the hip fits into the socket, and that tightness squishes the hip joint together, grinding down the joint surfaces. Living life with a rotated pelvis, walking, cooking, and exercising, the hip joint is constantly rubbing the wrong way because it doesn't fit together right. Over time that grinding can contribute to arthritis and hip joint issues.

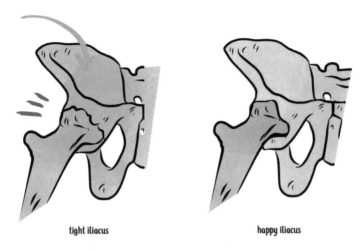

tight iliacus   happy iliacus

Anterior rotation of pelvis contributing to hip
arthritis and joint irritation

Hip arthritis is an inflamed, painful, and worn down hip joint. This condition is a huge phenomenon; 25 percent of us will experience painful hip arthritis in our lifetime (Murphy et al., 2010). There's a one in four chance this will happen to you, leading to hip replacement surgery later in life. Moving around with a tight iliacus significantly increases your chance of this happening. Helping to prevent hip arthritis and future surgery is reason enough for keeping that iliacus muscle relaxed and happy.

Inside the hip socket is a special type of joint surface called a labrum. The labrum helps to hold the ball in the socket. The suction created by a healthy labrum keeps the joint working well, decreasing the force going through the joint and keeping it well protected. Good suction in the joint happens when the ball and the socket line up well and the labrum isn't torn. If the alignment of the socket is off because the iliacus is tight, you can imagine the labrum being irritated and susceptible to tearing. Whether doing activities of daily life or athletic endeavors, moving with a ball that isn't fitting correctly into the socket also rubs the labrum the wrong way.

Labrum pain, as well as hip arthritis or joint pain, usually manifests as pain in the groin area. Similarly, iliopsoas tightness, or iliopsoas tendon issues, results in pain and discomfort in the groin. One symptom can be related to many causes. Therefore, it is important to release the tension in the iliopsoas and create a healthy environment for that muscle during a quest to decrease groin pain as that muscle might be the actual cause of the pain, not the joint.

Even if you have an X-ray or MRI that shows hip arthritis or labrum issues, it may not be the cause of your pain. There have been many studies that have shown that people can have arthritis amongst many other joint and tissue damage and, at the same time, not have any pain. Thirty-five percent of collegiate basketball players with no knee pain have significant abnormalities on an MRI (Major and Helms, 2002). Approximately one-third of total knee replacement surgeries are judged as inappropriate (Riddle, et al., 2014). Over the age of seventy, two out of three people have a rotator cuff tear with no pain (Milgrom, et al. 1995), and 40 percent of all people with no shoulder pain have a rotator cuff tear. In another study, 73 percent of people with no pain had abnormal hip joints, with 69 percent of them having a torn labrum (Register et al., 2012). The list goes on. Pain doesn't mean something is broken, and something broken doesn't equal pain.

You can start to see that even if you have hip arthritis, that doesn't mean that it is the source of your pain. Similarly, we cannot assume that if you have a torn hip labrum that it is the source of your pain. Anytime there's a pain in the hip area, you need to ask, "Is it caused by this arthritis that we're seeing on the X-ray? Is it caused by irritation of the labrum that we're seeing on this MRI? Or is it caused by some of the structures that are around those joints, like a tight iliopsoas?" Maybe the joint is just out of alignment due to a tight iliacus causing the pelvis to rotate.

I have treated quite a few people who have been diagnosed with labrum tears as well as hip arthritis. I've had great success reducing their pain and symptoms by simply releasing the tension in the iliacus muscle because, in fact, most of what they were experiencing in terms of symptoms was due to the iliacus muscle being constantly tight. Once we put prolonged pressure on the muscle to relax it, the tension and associated pain in the groin went away.

You can see here how tightness in the iliacus can cause irritation to the hip joint and create hip arthritis and issues with the labrum. You can also see how pain that is blamed on arthritis and hip labrum problems could actually be a result of tightness in the iliacus. This highlights the importance of treating that muscle, making it really loose and happy, before we jump to any conclusions of having surgeries, injections, or interventions to the hip joint or labrum itself.

Tight All Over

A tight iliacus initiates a war, causing tightness all over the hip region. I mentioned earlier how people focus so much on psoas tightness, releasing and stretching the psoas, and often forget about the iliacus. Because they live right next door to each other and connect to the same place on the thigh bone, when one is tight, the other is likely tight too. People who are experiencing symptoms that look like psoas tightness may actually have iliacus tightness. Without addressing the tightness of the iliacus itself, the psoas symptoms may not resolve. It's important to look at both of those muscles and make sure that they're both happy.

When any muscle is chronically tight, it's endlessly pulling on both of its endpoints. That pulling creates pain in the muscle belly itself and at the locations on the bone where it attaches. Both iliacus and psoas attach to the front of the hip near the groin area, and the iliacus attaches inside the pelvic bone and the psoas on the spine. Any of those points where they attach to the bone can develop into tendonitis (an irritated tendon) or bursitis (an irritated sac of fluid) from that muscle being constantly tight. You can address the inflammation in the tendon or bursa through physical therapy, movement, ice, or anti-inflammatory modes, but if the tightness of those muscles is not reduced, there's still going to be that constant pulling on that attachment point. Only when the tension in the muscle is released can the tension at the attachment be relieved and therefore the tendonitis or bursitis resolved.

Some surgeons offer an iliopsoas release surgery as a solution for a tight iliopsoas. This involves cutting the iliopsoas in an attempt to lessen the tension in that muscle. This is offered to people with pain and chronic tension in that muscle and failed treatments. Snipping all or part of that muscle seems like a necessary solution because the iliopsoas just won't relax. The tools and methods in the book should eliminate this type of surgery. Cutting a muscle whose primary job is to hold the top and bottom of the body together will really affect the stability of the core. Instead, by releasing the tension in the iliacus and psoas muscles with prolonged pressure, and learning how to prevent that tension from happening, this situation can be easily resolved without surgery.

Last, but not least, there is the effect on the back of the hip, the glute area. There are a bunch of muscles in the back of the hip that are the Villains to the iliopsoas, such as the glute, hamstring, piriformis, and deep hip rotator muscles, including obturator internus. They are the muscles that oppose the iliopsoas muscle on the other side of the pelvis and love the game of tug-of-war. If there is tension in the iliopsoas muscle itself, and the pelvis is being pulled forward, these muscles in the back of the hip will get tight and angry in revolt, causing pain and tightness in the gluteal area. Many of the muscles in the glute area connect to the thigh bone on the outside of the hip (greater trochanter). When there is constant tightness in one or more of these Villain muscles, the tug on this bony spot can get irritated, causing tendonitis or bursitis on that outside of the hip as well. Similarly, the inner thigh muscles (adductors) that attach to the pubic bone can also get tight or irritated when the pelvis is rotated or when the hip joint is irritated. This can all be traced to tightness in the iliacus muscle itself.

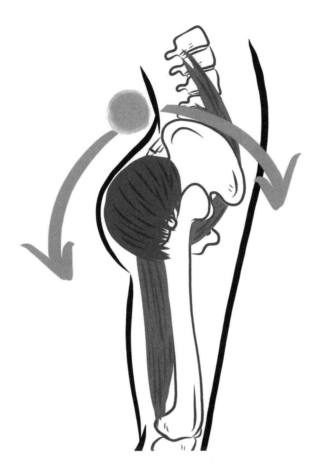

Tight iliopsoas playing tug-of-war with the glute,
piriformis, deep hip rotators, and hamstring

Tightness in the back of the hip and the iliopsoas makes it hard to move. Athletic endeavors that require a lot of hip motion, such as kicking, lunging, and squatting, are impacted. Daily activities such as reaching to the ground, sexual positions, and sitting on the ground become difficult. A strong and relaxed hip region allows for the body to function normally without constantly "feeling it" in the hip.

Making a Move

Having a tight iliopsoas affects the movement of the hip. One common example is going from sitting for a long time, where the iliopsoas is in a cramped position, to standing and asking that cramped muscle to lengthen, causing pain in the groin area. Similarly, a marching motion, such as climbing up a hill or stairs, uses an unhappy iliopsoas and can hurt. A tight iliopsoas does not always hurt to use, however. Tightness can be lurking below the surface, only noticed when the muscle is touched or the pelvis is rotated. This is how it has become such a hidden source of pain.

Marching and getting up from sitting can be painful
with an angry iliopsoas

A pinch in the hip when the knee is squeezed tightly to the chest is commonly attributed to hip arthritis or a hip labrum issue; however, it can also result from a tight iliacus. The anterior rotation of the pelvis from a tight iliacus changes the location of the hip socket, decreasing the available range of motion for the hip joint, so that when you bring the knee to the chest, it doesn't have as much space to fully flex. Sometimes, however, that pinch in the hip is not related to hip alignment, arthritis, or labrum issues, but an actual pinching of the iliopsoas where it is attached right up against the hip joint. When a muscle is holding tension, it takes up more space because the muscle is "on." For example, if you contract your bicep muscle, it gets bigger and takes up more space. When the iliopsoas muscle is tight and knotted it is easier to pinch because it is in the way. When you release the tension, that pinch goes away. You can tell if the iliopsoas and the associated rotation of the socket of the hip is to blame for this kind of pinching. Release the tension in the muscle and realign the pelvis (part of "3 Simple Steps") and then retest the knee to chest motion. If you can go further without a pinch or the pinch goes away completely, then the iliacus is at least partially responsible.

See if you get a pinch in your groin when you squeeze one knee at a time to your chest. When the pelvis is rotated forward, the joint has less space to flex.

With a tight iliopsoas, the hip will often pop or snap. This snapping sound can occur when a muscle flips over a bone. If the muscle is contracted, it behaves like a tight rubber band, and when you move, that tight rubber band flicks over a bone in the vicinity with a "snap." These pops can also occur because the hip joint is not fitting well in the socket. This kind of joint clunk often occurs lying down, lowering the legs down to the ground from the leg straight above. This kind of motion is a part of many Pilates and core exercises and is an indication of a tight iliacus. Because that tight muscle affects the alignment of the hip joint, the hip can shift in the socket and create a clunking noise. This can happen in other activities as well, such as triangle pose or extended hand to big toe pose in yoga. Ginger Garner, PT (integrativelifestylemed.com) has some additional online resources on the snapping hip and its many causes.

A "clunk" coming from the hip as the leg is lowered could be a sign of a tight iliopsoas

The moral of the story is that the hip needs to be properly situated in its socket in order for it to move properly and not clunk around. Because the iliopsoas attaches so close to the joint and affects the alignment of the hip joint itself, it's very common to have hip area issues as a result of this tight muscle. Making sure that the iliacus is relaxed and happy is key to a healthy hip.

...Thigh Bone

When a tight iliacus causes an anterior rotation, the effect down the chain begins. The thigh bone (femur) rotates inward, contributing to leg pain itself. This pain can be due to nerves, muscles, or referral patterns into the thigh.

You Are Not on a Roll

- IT band issues

Getting on My Nerves
- Nerve Pain
- Sciatica

Even Steven
- Hamstring issues
- Quad pain

Long Legs
- Leg length differences

You Are Not on a Roll

The anteriorly rotated pelvis changes the alignment of the ball in the socket, rotating the thigh bone inward. The muscles attached to the pelvis and the thigh bone don't like that. One of these affected muscles is a Sidekick, TFL (tensor fasciae latae). This small muscle attaches to the IT (iliotibial) band, a long piece of connective tissue that travels down the outside of the leg. A tight TFL pulls on the IT band and irritates it. Trying to fix the IT band itself by stretching it or rubbing it is a futile attempt because the issue is really coming from the TFL pulling on it, which all starts from the iliacus tightening up. If those muscles are not released, the IT band symptoms will not go away.

In many gyms and homes it is common to see people grimacing while rolling their IT bands on foam rollers. This is an endless treatment that does not get at the actual cause, but it does really hurt, giving the illusion that it's "good for you." I have never met anyone who actually rolled their IT band on a foam roller or any other device and was able to resolve those symptoms for good with that method. What I do see is people "rolling out" their IT bands day in and day out, self-inflicting pain without any long-term improvement. Just because it hurts to rub doesn't mean it's good for you.

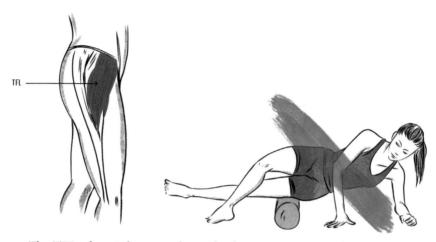

TFL

The TFL often tightens with a tight iliopsoas irritating the IT band; however, rolling the IT band is not only aggravating, it is also not addressing the cause of its irritation.

If the actual cause of the IT band soreness is not resolved, such as the tight iliacus or TFL, the IT band will stay irritated. The IT band itself is a piece of connective tissue, and its goal is to hold things together and to be tight. It does not need to be flexible, stretched out, or massaged. It's not a muscle that is to be stretched, it's a piece of connective tissue. If we stopped rolling and trying to "break up the adhesions" in the IT band and really looked at what's causing it to be irritated in the first place, we would save much time with less wincing.

Getting on My Nerves

Similar to the referral phenomenon of trigger points, there are quite a few nerves that run through and near the iliopsoas, and when those nerves get pinched by a tight muscle, they can also refer symptoms. Nerves do not like to be pulled on or pinched and will cause referral pain if they are not happy. The referral pattern diagrams for the nerves near the iliopsoas will help you to determine if an unhappy nerve may be responsible for your issue.

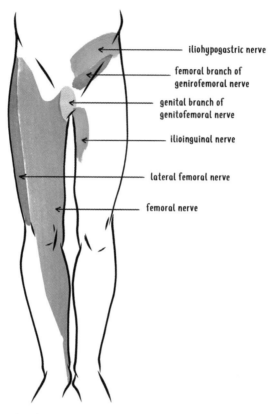

Nerves near the iliopsoas can get irritated when that muscle is tight,
causing these referral patterns

Sciatic pain is another nerve-related condition that plagues 40 percent of all adults at some point in their lives, causing nerve pain into the glute, leg, shin, and foot (Ergun and Lakadamyali, 2010). When the psoas and iliacus are tight, the lower back goes into extension, side-bending, and rotation, decreasing the space for the nerve to come out of the spine and down the leg. Additionally, a tight iliacus pulls the pelvis forward and causes tightness in the piriformis muscle on the back of the hip. The sciatic nerve travels right through or under this muscle. The combination of a smaller space for the nerve to exit the spine and a tight piriformis pinching on the nerve create a perfect storm for the development of sciatica. By addressing the tension and tightness in the iliacus and the psoas muscle and getting the pelvis back into alignment, the piriformis will relax and the nerve will have more space. This will give that sciatic nerve an opportunity to heal and stop creating a pain in the leg.

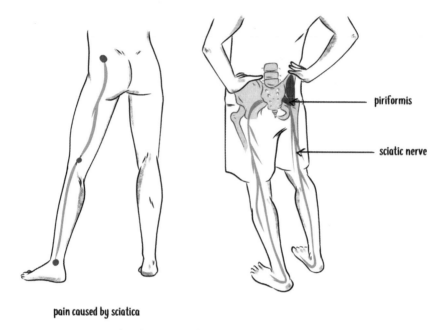

piriformis

sciatic nerve

pain caused by sciatica

An anterior rotated pelvis contributes to pinched nerves in the spine and a tight piriformis, contributing to sciatic pain down the leg

Pain can be referred to other parts of the body not only by nerves, but also by trigger points and organs. The trigger points that commonly refer to areas like the thigh, hip, and back can be found in Part 4 under "Release Neighboring Tight Spots." Pain that looks like nerve pain can also be trigger point pain, so it's important to check that as well. Trigger points can easily develop in the Sidekicks and Villain muscles, creating these kinds of phenomenon.

Even Steven

Because the iliacus pulls the pelvis forward and the job of the hamstring is to pull the pelvis backward, tug-of-war is just waiting to happen. The attachment of the hamstring, which is right on the sit bone, can also get irritated, developing into hamstring tendonitis. This effect can be amplified if excessive hamstring stretching is done while having a tight iliacus, very common in yoga. Over time this pulling wears away at that attachment point on the sit bone, causing pain there or in the muscle belly.

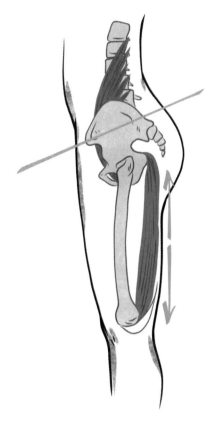

An anteriorly rotated pelvis from a tight iliopsoas
tugs on the hamstring

On the front side of the leg lives the quad (quadriceps). Part of this muscle helps the iliopsoas muscle to flex the hip, acting as a Sidekick. It attaches right in the front of the pelvic bone, very near where the iliacus and the psoas attach on the front of the hip. If the pelvis is rotated, the quad gets into a shortened position and that can cause tightness or pain in the quad itself. That tight quad may be hard to stretch and can be weak as a result; remember, tight and short muscles are weak muscles. There are also trigger points in the iliopsoas that will refer pain down into this area. Sometimes quad pain can be a result of the trigger point up north in the iliopsoas muscle itself.

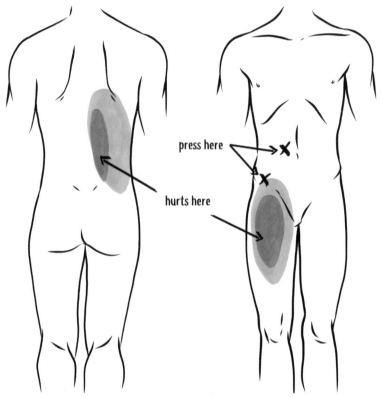

press here

hurts here

Trigger points in the iliacus and psoas can refer to the thigh and the mid to lower back

Long Legs

Many people have been told that one leg is longer than the other and have been given special orthotics or heel lifts to put in one shoe to help even that out. Although some people are born with one thigh bone longer than the other or sometimes a knee or hip surgery creates one leg longer than the other, this is rare. Most people really have what's called a functional length difference. This is where one leg *seems* longer because of the way the muscles are pulling on the bones, not because the bones themselves are different sizes.

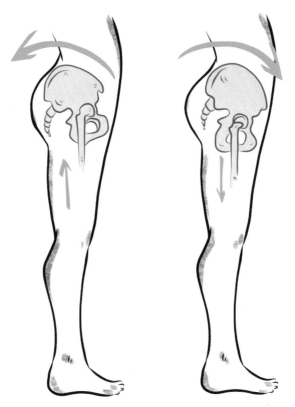

An anterior rotated pelvis on one side makes that leg appear longer

On the side of the body where the iliacus is tight, in standing, that leg will seem longer. This will often make the foot on that side flatter, as the body is trying to adjust. Heel lifts placed in the opposite shoe to even out this temporary leg length difference is treating the symptom and not the cause. You can double-check the temporary nature in tall sitting—that same leg that is longer in standing will seem shorter in long sitting with a functional leg length difference.

If the iliacus is relaxed, and the pelvis is in alignment, then the length of that leg can return to normal, both in standing and tall sitting. It's important any time you have a leg length difference to make sure the real cause is being addressed because if a heel lift is added to a leg that really isn't short, it can throw off the entire body. There are many other alignment issues with the spine and pelvis that can contribute to a functional leg length difference and those should also be addressed before correcting with a lift. A physical therapist, chiropractor, or osteopath who specializes in spinal alignment is your greatest ally in figuring out the true cause of a leg length difference.

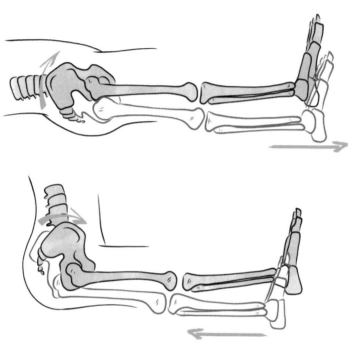

...Knee Joint

The inwardly rotated thigh bone as a result of a tight iliacus changes the way the knee works. This rotation twists the inside surfaces of the knee joint and irritates the structures around the knee. The hip is the first place I look when a knee issue arises as it is so commonly a cause.

The Leaning Tower of Bones

- MCL and adductor issues
- Knee arthritis
- Meniscus issues

Lost My Groove

- Kneecap (patellofemoral) pain

The Leaning Tower of Bones

A tight iliacus results in a thigh bone rotated inward relative to the shin bone, causing a stretch and strain to the inside of the knee. Structures like the MCL (medial collateral ligament) and the nearby inner thigh (adductor) muscles strain and inflame. Stretch to the inside of the knee puts more pressure on the outside of the knee, contributing to arthritis and wear in that lateral part of the knee. This twist in the knee can also strain the meniscus in both sides of the knee and set the body up for a meniscus strain or tear. The meniscus, similar to the labrum in the hip, is a special type of cartilage on the surface of the knee joint that helps to absorb shock in the knee and keep it stable. In the same way that the ball needs to fit well into the hip socket, our knee joints need to line up well in order for them to not wear down. The knee just doesn't line up right when the iliacus is tight and the thigh bone is rotated inward.

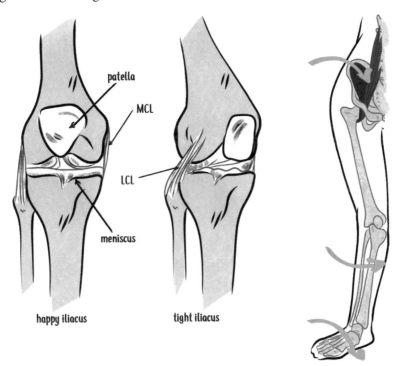

happy iliacus   tight iliacus

An anteriorly rotated pelvis causes an inwardly rotated
femur and strains the knee

Lost My Groove

The patellofemoral joint consists of the kneecap (patella) and the thigh bone (femur). In a healthy knee, the kneecap glides smoothly in a groove in the thigh bone when the knee is bent and straightened. With a rotated thigh bone, this groove is out of place, making the kneecap lose its groove, causing wear and pain. Irritation and wear can occur to the underside of the kneecap or on the thigh bone itself. It can even cause irritation to the tendon below the kneecap, where it attaches to the shin bone. By correcting the alignment of the thigh bone by releasing the pull that the iliacus is producing, the kneecap can get back in its groove.

Many efforts have been made to align the kneecap to recover from pain and wear, including braces, orthotics, tape, and joint manipulations. These only offer temporary results if indeed the iliacus is the prime cause of the rotated pelvis and knee irritation. When releasing the tension in the iliacus muscle, the pelvis aligns, the leg rotates back into place, and the knee returns to working properly, helping these issues to resolve.

...Foot Bones

Working its way to the end of the chain, the effect of the iliacus is strong in the foot. That internal rotation of the leg turns into a twisted ankle and flattened foot. It even twists the toes.

- Ankle pinch
- Achilles strain
- Plantar fasciitis
- Overpronation
- Bunion
- Shoe wear complications

As the tight iliacus initiates a train wreck from the pelvis to the shin, the ankle turns inward and the foot gets flatter. If the bones in the foot don't line up properly they can cause ankle wear that sometimes shows up like a pinch in the ankle. You don't want to make a wrong step! The Achilles tendon can also be strained because the tendon is twisted a little bit in this position.

Because the foot becomes flatter (pronation) with a tight iliacus, the bottom of the foot can get irritated and can cause something called plantar fasciitis, or arch pain. Arch pain is a huge problem for many athletes, especially runners. With tightness in the iliopsoas being so common in runners, it is easy to see how the resulting rotated pelvis contributing to overpronation can be a factor. The tissue on the bottom of the foot is stressed too much with all of that force from the sport in combination with the effects of the rotation.

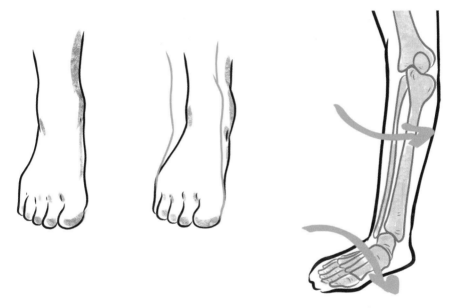

An anteriorly rotated pelvis causes the foot to flatten and strains the arch and ankle area

The big toe, because of the pronation, ends up being more pointed towards the other toes, ultimately changing the walking pattern, walking over the inside of the foot, rolling over the toe. Over time this can develop into a bunion. These changes in the mechanics of the foot that all started in the hip affect the wear pattern on shoes and may cause calluses or shoe irritations.

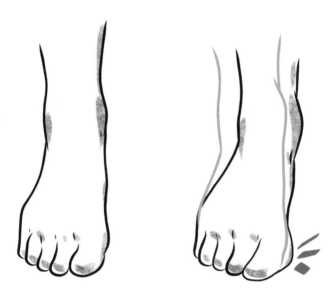

Overpronation from an anteriorly rotated pelvis contributes
to bunion development

It doesn't seem like the iliopsoas would be related to what's happening at the foot, but in fact, it's very closely related. Releasing the tension in the iliopsoas and getting the pelvis back into alignment allow for a better alignment of the leg and shin, with less pronation at the foot and less irritation to all of those structures in the foot that don't like to be stretched and twisted.

...Diaphragm

Our diaphragm is a muscle responsible for breathing; its importance is no joke. When the diaphragm contracts, it pulls air into the lungs by creating more space in the chest cavity and less space in the abdomen. That's why you can feel your stomach expand when you take a deep breath. Breathing using your chest instead does not facilitate relaxation and we are unable to fully get the oxygen we need, and our stress level will increase. Stress is correlated to the frequency of deep abdominal breaths, and a tight iliopsoas makes that type of breath difficult.

- Difficulty breathing
- Vagus nerve and sympathetic nervous system
- Rib and abdominal pain

Because the psoas muscle is attached to all of the lower (lumbar) spine bones (vertebrae) all the way up to the connection to the rib cage, tightness in the psoas affects the diaphragm. In fact, the connective tissue that surrounds the iliacus and the inside of the pelvic bowl runs up the back of the spine to the psoas and then blends with the diaphragm. This makes a big "C" shape. This is part of the deep front line that Thomas W. Myers outlines so eloquently in his book *Anatomy Trains: Myofascial Meridians for Manual and Movement Therapists*. When there are restrictions and tension in the psoas or iliacus muscle it will pull on the diaphragm itself.

The ability to manage stress is orchestrating a delicate balance between the sympathetic nervous system (fight and flight) and the parasympathetic nervous system (rest and digest). Part of the sympathetic nervous system travels along the psoas, correlating to a strong connection between the health of the psoas and the stress response. Part of the parasympathetic nervous system is the vagus nerve, and the vagus nerve travels through the diaphragm. Vagus nerve activity is affected by breathing, working the best during exhalation and slow deep breaths (Chang et al., 2015). A well functioning vagus nerve improves heart rate variability, an indicator of resilience to stress, physical conditioning, and general health.

When the diaphragm is not able to take full, deep, slow breaths, the vagus nerve isn't stimulated properly. This rest and digest function is essential to our ability to digest our food, repair our body, fight infection, detoxify, and decrease inflammation. When we take just three deep breaths into the abdomen, it helps to shift us from the fight or flight to rest and digest, helping to regain calm and these essential body functions. The degree of ease in taking those deep breaths is directly related to the alignment of the diaphragm, which is directly impacted by tension in the psoas and the iliacus muscle.

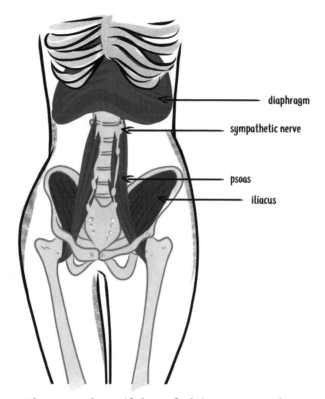

The sympathetic (fight or flight) nerves travel
right next to the psoas.

Also, when people have tension in the iliopsoas, they will
experience something that feels like rib pain or abdominal pain. The
tug of those muscles affects the bones around them. There are a lot of
different structures in the area that could be the cause of abdominal or
rib pain. It's very important to see a doctor and rule out any possible
issues with the organs. It's also possible that the pain is coming from
tension in the iliopsoas pulling on all that's around it.

...Upper Body

The rotation in the lower back and pelvis from a tight iliopsoas can
work its way all the way up the spine, affecting the alignment of the
bones all the way up to the head. This can affect the alignment of the

ribs, shoulders, neck, and finally, the head, resulting in pain or tightness along the way. Looking at the whole body is key, even when addressing something as far away as the hip and the head.

- Rib cage twist
- Shoulder issues
- Neck and head pain

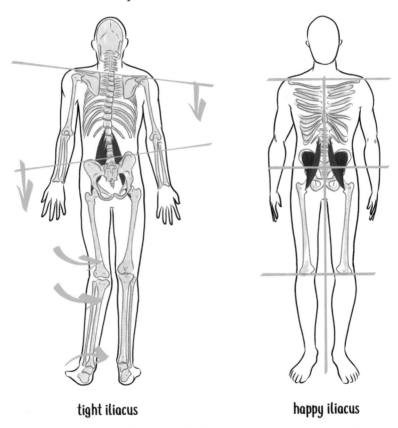

tight iliacus   happy iliacus

A rotated pelvis from a tight iliopsoas works its way up the spine to the ribs, shoulders, and neck

The pelvis is the foundation for the rest of the body. If it is not aligned, the rest of the body compensates in a multitude of ways, as we have seen. Each individual has their weakest link for where the tight iliopsoas will show up. Maybe it is in the hip itself, in the big toe, or as a headache. Regardless of the result, you can see how important having a relaxed and happy iliopsoas is to the overall health of the body. Keeping this area from getting tight and releasing it when it does get tight go a long way to keeping your body functioning at its best.

Out of Balance

Just by being tight, the iliacus changes the length of the hamstring, quad, psoas, glute, inner thigh, piriformis, deep hip rotators, back, and TFL muscles, and directly or indirectly all the other muscles up and down the chain. When a muscle is not at its ideal length, it doesn't work well. One of two things will happen. When a muscle is too short for its taste, it easily develops muscle knots and gets weak, unable to contract at its full strength. When a muscle is too long for its design, it has a hard time contracting at all and becomes weak, sometimes tightening with fear that it might get lengthened more, losing even more power.

As you can see, once something is out of alignment, every muscle that's related to that area can be affected through decreased strength or decreased flexibility. For example, if the iliacus is tight, the piriformis muscle often feels sore when you stretch it because, as a Villain to the iliopsoas, it's playing tug-of-war. It is already being pulled on by the iliacus and then it is being asked to stretch even more; it's unlikely to give in. Once the iliacus is relaxed, the piriformis isn't being bothered anymore, reducing its soreness and allowing for more motion when it is stretched. Similarly, weakness in the glute can be a result of tightness in the iliopsoas because the glute gets stretched beyond its normal length and has a hard time generating the force it's capable of at its ideal length.

The question arises once again: is it the chicken or the egg? Often, weakness in the hips or weakness in some of the muscles around the core can contribute to an easily tightened iliopsoas. For example, if you don't have strength in your deep abdominal muscles, your pelvis will tend to be rotated more forward. As a result of that, the iliacus is going to be in a more shortened position, easily causing it to develop a knot. The iliacus and psoas also have to work a lot harder when you don't have the strength in the core muscles like the lower back and the abdominal and hip muscles, working a lot harder to hold everything together.

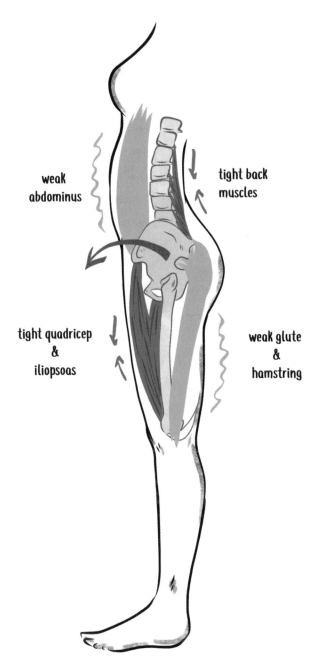

weak
abdominus

tight back
muscles

tight quadricep
&
iliopsoas

weak glute
&
hamstring

An anteriorly rotated pelvis shortens and tightens in the back muscles, iliopsoas, and quadricep. At the same time it lengthens and weakens the hamstring, glute, and abdominal muscles.

Interestingly, flexibility imbalances can also be related to more tightness in one iliopsoas over the other. For example, in dancers with one hamstring more flexible, allowing for a higher kick, the opposite iliacus is often found to be tight. Over years of working to stretch the tighter hamstring loose, a simple releasing of the iliacus can instantly result in more range of motion and a higher kick.

Another interesting pattern I've observed in my decades of physical therapy practice is more right-sided iliacus tightness then left-sided. Ninety percent of my clients who have tight iliacus muscles tend to have tightness on their right side with a right forward (anterior) rotated pelvis, with the other 10 percent left-sided. I've also noticed that most people that I treat who have had a knee or hip replacement tend to have more right-sided replacements then left. This observation is possibly just anecdotal, but I've always wondered if there's some sort of correlation between tightness in the iliacus and the development of hip and knee arthritis on that same side. This correlation makes sense to me! Tightness in the iliopsoas muscle affects the orientation of the hip joint, which affects how the knee is aligned, and can really contribute to rubbing the hip and knee the wrong way.

It is possible that as humans we use our bodies a certain way that causes right-sided tightness and issues more often. Maybe it has something to do with driving, handedness, the inherent asymmetries of our innards, or the effects of the location we live on the globe. I've been asking these questions for decades and would love to see someone do some research on the topic. Who knows, maybe the answer to preventing hip and knee arthritis lies in that question.

Regardless of which side, 99 percent of the time there will be more tightness on one side than the other, creating an imbalance in the body. It is rare to have equal tightness on both the right and the left iliacus. The body is never going to be perfectly balanced, no matter what we do, but working towards balance absolutely improves the health and function of the body. When severe imbalances occur, the body will not move well.

Is it the Chicken or the Egg?

As you may have noticed, there are quite a few phenomena in the body that can cause or be caused by a tight iliopsoas. As with the age-old conundrum of the chicken or the egg, we will never know which is primarily responsible. Is the hip arthritis causing the tight iliopsoas or is the tight iliopsoas causing the hip arthritis? Is the anteriorly rotated pelvis causing the foot overpronation or is the overpronation causing the anteriorly rotated pelvis? Is the back pain caused by the tight iliopsoas or is the tight iliopsoas causing the back pain?

Regardless what is primary, release of the tension in the iliopsoas and aligning the pelvis do help to break the cycle and keep the body functioning at its best. Even if an already established disease process, such as hip dysplasia, is creating tightness in these muscles, it is still prudent to help keep those muscles happy so that the rest of the body can align and work properly, even if the release has to be repeated from time to time. The key to your health is a soft and supple hip that is aligned and setting the stage for the rest of the body to work as intended.

PART 4:
SOFTEN THE HIP TO
SOLVE YOUR PAIN

Have you been doing your exercises and stretches, heat and cold, tape and ultrasound, foam rolls and Theragun, without resolving your pain? Have you been seeing loads of health practitioners, resting up and scouring the internet for solutions, and still not getting better? This can mean only one thing. The real cause of the problem is not being addressed. Something is missing.

This is really simple. If you don't address the cause of your pain, your pain will not go away. That's why so many medications, surgeries, and treatments fail. They address the symptom but not the "why." For example, if you're working on helping your arch pain by placing an orthotic in your shoe, but the iliacus is still tight, it's still going to put pressure on the arch and that orthotic is not going to be enough.

Releasing the iliacus works. Up until now, this has been an area that has been hard to access and missed as a crucial component of recovery. There has been no standard technique to get into that muscle and actually apply an effective amount of pressure on it. Furthermore, there has been no examination of the role of this muscle as a cause of pain in other places, even though its role is clearly impactful. Releasing that hard to reach muscle may be what it takes to address the actual cause of your pain.

If you have had your iliacus treated before with a pressure release technique, then you are a unicorn. If you are not a unicorn, then tightness in this muscle has likely never been assessed or addressed for you. That muscle has likely never been touched at all. To be clear, I'm not claiming every issue has the iliacus at its core. But if you haven't tried making your iliacus happy, you may be surprised to find that you do actually get better and that you *have* been a unicorn all along.

QUIZ: Do You Have a Tight Iliacus?

Now is the time to find out if a tight iliopsoas is a problem for *you*. Take this quiz to see if you are one of the masses of humans with tightness in this area. By tallying the right and the left side, you will be able to tell which side is tightest as well. This will come in handy in the next section where we reveal what to do about it. Check the boxes that apply to you using the illustrations as a guide.

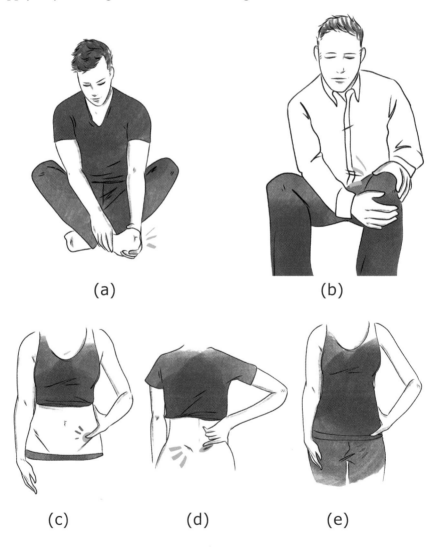

(a)

(b)

(c)

(d)

(e)

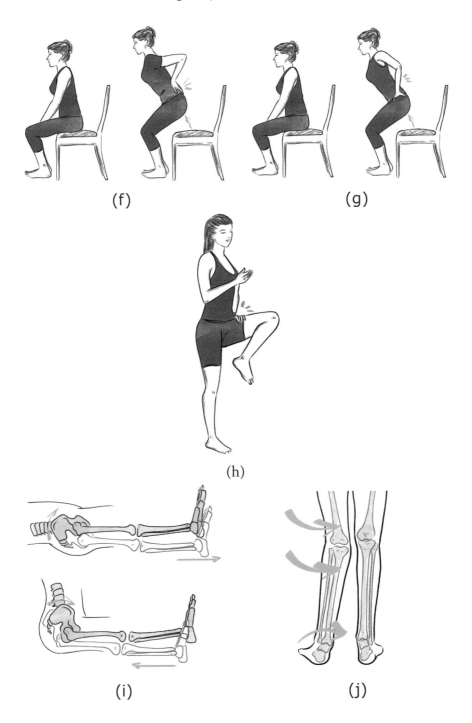

(f)

(g)

(h)

(i)

(j)

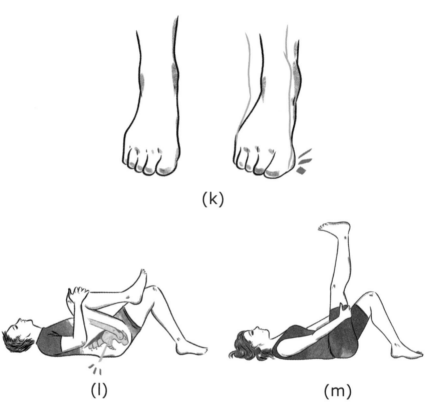

(k)

(l)   (m)

(n)

	Right side	Left side	Unsure
Hurts on bottom of foot (a)			
Hurts on inside of knee (b)			
Hurts to rub front of hip bone (ASIS) (c)			
Hurts to rub SI (sacroiliac) joint (d)			
Hurts in groin area during daily life (e)			
Hurts in groin when standing up from sitting a while (f)			
Hurts in low back when standing up from sitting a while (g)			
Hurts to lift leg in a march (h)			
Which leg gets shorter going from lying down to sitting with legs straight? (i)			
Which arch is flatter in standing? (j)			

Which side has the worst bunion? (k)			
Which hip pinches in the groin when the knee is squeezed into the chest? (l)			
Which side has the tightest hamstring? (m)			
Which side pulls more in a lunge stretch? (n)			
Total each column			

Scoring:

- If you scored more than 2 on either side, right or left, you likely have a tight iliopsoas.
- The column with the highest total (right or left) is the side that is the tightest. If the total on one side is 2 points or more than the other side, it's likely that the iliacus on the winner side is a primary cause of your pain.
- If you can see that one leg gets shorter going from lying down to long sitting, then you know for sure that that is the side with the tightest iliacus as this is a sign for an anteriorly rotated pelvis.
- Make a note of which side has the highest score and therefore is the tightest as that will be useful as we unveil the "3 Simple Steps."

3 Simple Steps

In three simple steps, you can resolve the tension in the iliopsoas muscle and align the pelvis, allowing the body to function at its best.

Step 1: Release the Front of the Hip – This involves finding a technique that works for you to apply prolonged pressure to the iliacus muscle to release its tension, releasing any trigger points or knots contributing to its tightness.

Step 2: Release the Back of the Hip – This step focuses on releasing tension in the Villain muscles that play tug-of-war with the iliacus. Using prolonged pressure to the glute, piriformis, and deep rotators will achieve this.

Step 3: Realign the Pelvis – After releasing the tension that has been pulling the hips and pelvis out of line, this technique uses our own muscles to bring the pelvic bones back in place. You can do this in different positions: on your back, sitting, or standing.

Both Step 1 and Step 2 can only be achieved with prolonged pressure, not rolling, rubbing, or stretching. Prolonged pressure means finding the spot that is tight and holding mild to moderate pressure on that muscle until the tension in that muscle has lessened or goes away. The length of time needed for the muscle to let go will vary. Sometimes the tension and "pain" from the pressure will go away in thirty to ninety seconds; sometimes it may take longer to fully resolve. Being patient and watching the tension melt away is key. This technique is often called trigger point release.

When placing prolonged pressure on a muscle it should feel like a "hurts so good" kind of sensation, like a tight muscle has finally found someone to pay attention to it! It should not feel sharp or scary. If the pain doesn't feel right, stop. Take it slow. Remember, these muscles have probably never been worked on before and they have likely been tight for decades. I recommend having a healthcare professional press on the correct area first so that you can know what you are supposed to feel, helping you with accurate self-treatment.

After holding the constant, mild to moderate pressure on the muscle, you'll notice the intensity of the "hurts so good" sensation will become less and less as the muscle softens and relaxes. The tool that you are using to provide the pressure will then fall deeper into the muscle and, after a period of time, you won't feel like it's doing much of anything anymore. That's when you know that it's time to stop the pressure. If you don't feel it get less intense over time, then stop, something is not right. Feel free to experiment with moving the pressure point up or down a smidge to try a different angle; after all, these muscles are big and have quite a bit of surface to cover.

The release exercises are done once a day. Maybe even once every other day. When you first start pressing on a muscle that is tight and hasn't been pressed on before, it might be pretty sore. It's not uncommon to feel sore right after doing these releases initially, even the next day. If you do feel sore, give yourself a break and let yourself recover until that soreness goes away. Then you can resume the release when you are ready. No rush. As you progress, and you've been tolerating it well, you can do the releases daily. If you're doing an activity that is making your iliacus tight, you may want to release it before and after that activity; for example, before and after sitting all day at work.

Using these methods does not have to be a lifelong process. If you work at it constantly for two to three weeks, you will notice great change. Once the muscle has learned how to relax and the pelvis is in its correct spot, then you can use these tools occasionally as a tune-up, once a week or as needed.

Step 1: Release the Front of the Hip

We have talked over and over about how a tight iliacus could be impacting your life. Now it's time to do something about it! The ultimate goal is to find a way to put prolonged pressure on the iliacus muscle to get that muscle to stop holding tension and to release any knots or trigger points in that muscle. The importance of prolonged pressure was discussed in "Pressure is the Golden Ticket," just in case you forgot.

You may ask, what about the psoas? Shouldn't we release that too? It is true, when the iliacus is tight, the psoas is often, but not always, tight. When you use the techniques outlined below, you will also be releasing the tension in the psoas. The iliacus and psoas lie on top of each other at the location where pressure is applied when using the Hip Hook or the ball. After that initial pressure is placed, we then turn to inside the pelvis to get at the iliacus specifically. This is the benefit of the Hip Hook or a trained manual therapist over other tools—the ability to address both the iliacus and psoas at the same time. Also, in my experience, releasing the iliacus seems to also soften the tension of the psoas, leaving releasing the psoas on its own unnecessary most of the time.

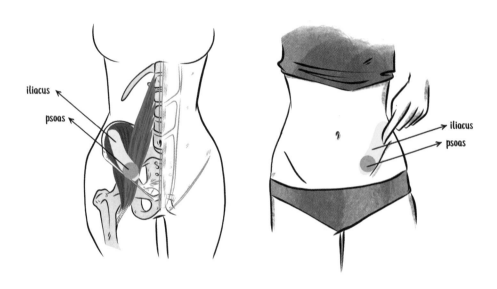

The sweet spot to release the iliopsoas

Use the Hip Hook

Over decades of practice, I have not found a single tool that one can use on their own to release the iliacus. Balls, rollers, kettlebells, canes, remote controls, or spatulas do not work. I've tried them all. This problem has remained unsolved until my invention of the Hip Hook. This is the *only* way to access and release the iliacus without the help of a friend. This tool was expertly designed to replicate the pressure on the iliacus muscle that only a skilled practitioner could produce. It's designed with the exact right angle, tip, and leverage for the job.

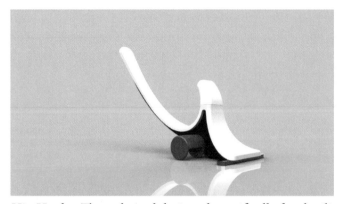

The Hip Hook—The only tool designed specifically for the iliacus

Using the Hip Hook involves three simple steps: NIP, HIP, TIP.

NIP: Lie on your side with the targeted hip on top.
Line up the tip of the Hip Hook to your nipple.

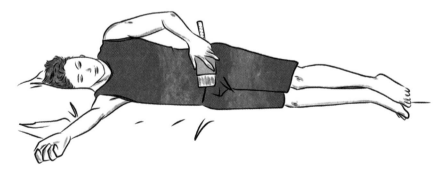

HIP: Slide the tip down to the hip.
Find the soft spot just inside the pelvic bone.

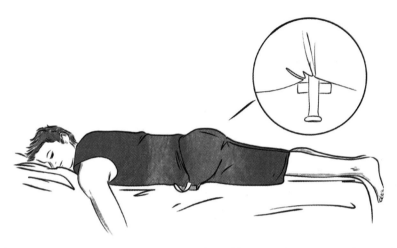

TIP: Tip your body onto the Hip Hook and let it sink into your iliacus. The iliacus is located in the soft spot right near the inside surface of the pelvic bone. Make sure the tip is pointing upward initially and the tool doesn't tip underneath you. You can move it around slightly underneath you to find the right spot as needed. Although it may feel good to use it lower down at the crease where your leg meets your pelvis, do not use it there. Place it in the soft spot near the inside surface of your pelvic bone.

Once you are positioned on top of the Hip Hook, let your body melt into the tool. At first the pressure might be intense, especially if you have never done this before. Remember, happy muscles don't hurt.

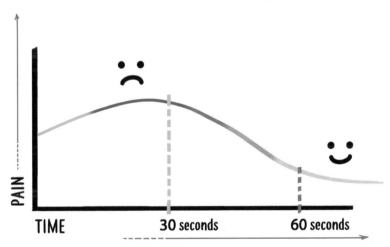

The initial pressure will be intense but over time it will decrease

After the initial pressure has lessened, use your hand to place a gentle downward pressure on the handle that's outside of the hip. This will allow for the tool to press towards the pelvic bone to where the iliacus attaches on the pelvic bone. Allow for the Hip Hook to put prolonged pressure on the muscle and feel it gradually relax.

Use your hand to press on the lever to provide pressure to the side where the iliacus lives

As mentioned above, hold the prolonged pressure for thirty to ninety seconds, whatever it takes for the soreness to lessen or disappear. You can do this on both sides. You only need to do this once a day or even once every other day. Make sure you read the above introduction in "3 Simple Steps" so you know how much pressure to use and what you should feel.

When you do this for the first time, it will be sore. After all, this muscle has never been touched before and it's been tight for ages. It will get better over time. Take it slow. If you get sore, take a break for a day or two. It will get easier. If it feels painful in a not so good way, stop.

There are many positions that you can play with to release the iliacus. Try these out once you've become comfortable with the technique. Try pressing up onto your elbows or hands, squeezing your glutes together, bending your knee and swinging the foot side to side, bringing your opposite leg out to the side, bending and straightening your knee, and lifting your leg off the floor. Check out TheHipHook. com for more ideas on how to use this tool.

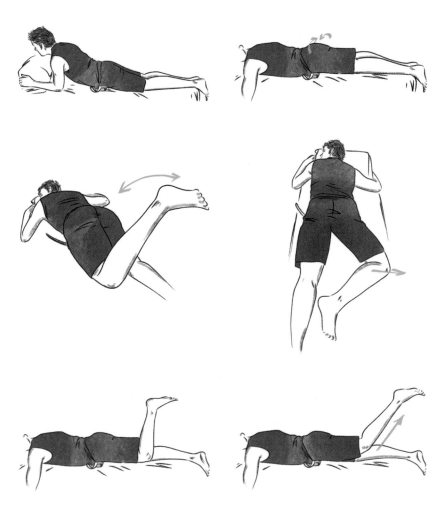

Different ways to explore access to the iliacus with the Hip Hook

Use a Ball

Although the ball cannot touch the iliacus muscle itself, it can get to the general area and create an effect that is therapeutic for the iliacus and psoas. Using a ball is also another way to start slowly with this release as the pressure is more subtle. Smaller balls do not work because they just get absorbed into the abdomen. A four-inch bouncy ball is ideal because it's tall enough to get into the region and hard enough to produce pressure (see "Resources").

Follow the instructions above for the Hip Hook (NIP, HIP, TIP) for placing the ball; it's the same location. Let the iliopsoas region relax on the ball by holding prolonged pressure for thirty to ninety seconds, whatever it takes for the soreness to disappear. You can do this on both sides. You only need to do this once a day or even once every other day. Make sure you read the above introduction in "3 Simple Steps" so you know how much pressure to use and what you should feel. Feel free to explore the different positions in the "Hip Hook" section above with the ball as your tool as well.

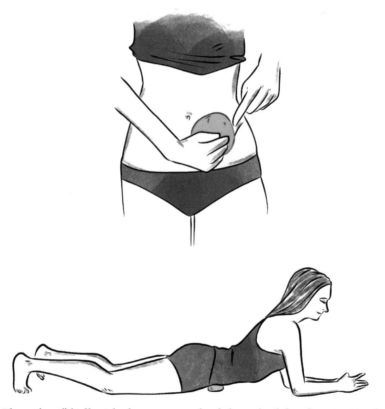

Place the 4" ball with the same method described for the Hip Hook

Use a Friend

Find a friend or healthcare practitioner to release the muscle for you. Make a friend if you don't have any, preferably one that can release this muscle or at least is willing to learn how to do it. Because of the location of the iliacus, it's nearly impossible to get the right angle and pressure using your own hands.

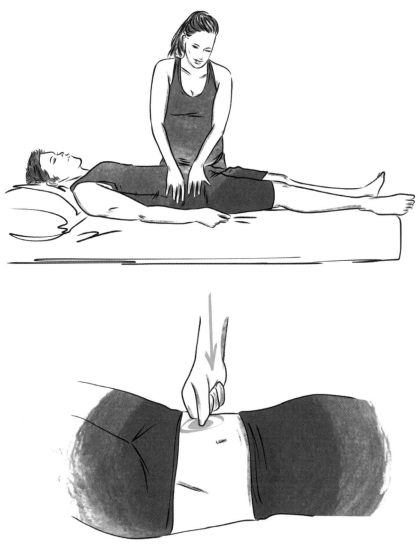

Another person can help you by putting prolonged pressure on the iliacus

The friend stands to the opposite side of your tight iliacus, placing their thumbs on the tip of the bone of your pelvis. Slowly let the thumbs glide to the inside surface of the pelvic bone, looking for sore and tight spots on the inside of the bone. Once a spot is found, stop and maintain prolonged pressure on that spot until the soreness dissipates or the friend feels the muscle soften under the thumbs. The most effective direction of the pressure is towards the bone, squeezing the muscle between their thumbs and the bone. Move the thumbs to the next tight spot and repeat.

Holding the prolonged pressure can take anywhere from thirty to ninety seconds, depending on how long it takes for the soreness to disappear. You can do this on both sides. By positioning the friend on the side opposite to the side being released, it's much easier for them to maintain sustained pressure and squeeze that muscle in the right direction against the bone.

Step 2: Release the Back of the Hip

After the iliacus is released, the back of your hip will be waiting for attention.

The soft area just to the side of your tailbone is the home to many muscles that get tight from pulling against the iliacus. The location of the pressure should be on the soft fleshy part to the side on the tailbone, not on the tailbone or spine itself. When the Villains are relaxed they won't be tugging on the iliacus anymore. Releasing the back of the hip is important for creating an environment for the iliacus to feel safe and stay relaxed too.

There are many types of tools, such as a tennis ball, racquetball, or foam roller, that can be put to good pressure on this glute area. My favorite tool is the four-inch bouncy ball because it is hard enough to produce pressure but it isn't too pointy in a sensitive area where lots of nerves live (see "Resources").

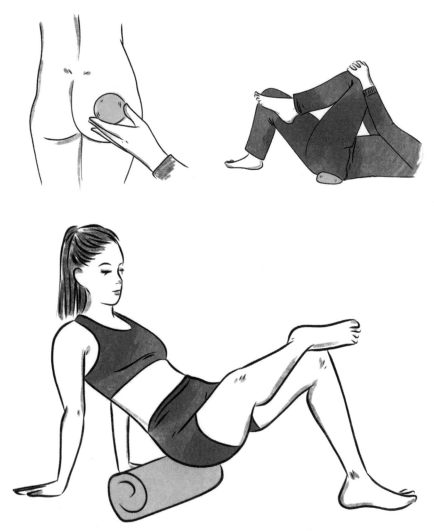

Methods for releasing the back of the hip

As mentioned above, hold the prolonged pressure for thirty to ninety seconds, whatever it takes for the soreness to lessen or disappear. You can do this on both sides. You only need to do this once a day or even once every other day. Make sure you read the above introduction in "3 Simple Steps" so you know how much pressure to use and what you should feel.

Step 3: Realign the Pelvis

After the tension in the iliacus and the Villains are released, it's time to put the pelvis back in place. Your body has likely been tight and out of alignment for a very long time. This exercise is retraining your pelvis to behave in an entirely new way. Just like a dog that is being trained, the commands must be repeated over and over. Eventually, the dog will learn to sit. The dog needs to practice sitting at home, when it sees a squirrel, with visitors, and at the dinner table in order to truly master sitting. Just like the dog, repetition in different scenarios and over time is needed to retrain the pelvis to hold the correct alignment.

There are certain times in your daily life that are ideal to do the realignment exercise. First thing in the morning and before bed bookmarks the day so that you start and end with an aligned pelvis. If you partake in any of these muscle releases, stretches, or exercises in this book, or any other stretches or exercises for that matter, realigning the pelvis after you've finished is ideal because there is a good chance what you have done has pulled you out of alignment.

Participating in any of the activities in the section "We All Have Tight Hips" will likely twist the core, another perfect time to realign the pelvis before and after those activities. Doing it before the activity puts the pelvis in proper alignment so that the muscles will work well and you don't create any irritation to the body. Completing the activity with the realignment exercise is like the icing on the cake. You've just done an activity that was challenging to the hips and there's a good chance that it might have pulled yourself out of alignment or tightened up your iliacus. It's a perfect time to get it back in place before you embark on the rest of the day.

As you can see, the pelvic realignment exercise should be done multiple times throughout the day. Again, we're training your body to hold your body into a new position. At first, ten times a day is ideal, working down to once a day when you're feeling better. There are different positions to realign the pelvis, so you can find various places throughout your day to get your ten repetitions in. The more frequent the exercise the more the body is going to remember where those bones should be. Remember, the iliacus muscle has been pulling the pelvis out of alignment for a very long time. It needs retraining.

This exercise works by contracting the glute and hamstring muscle to pull an anteriorly rotated pelvis back to a properly aligned pelvis. We are using the tug-of-war to our advantage. Secondarily, the muscle opposite a contracted muscle turns off. So by contracting the hamstring and glute we are urging the iliacus and psoas to relax. Like the intermittent pulling that is required to get a stuck dresser drawer unstuck, this exercise uses a two-second contraction and relaxation, repeated ten times, to achieve the effect. The various positions of the pelvis in this exercise allow the bone the freedom to rotate.

Important

This exercise is done on only one side. You must first decide which side of the body has the tightest iliacus and is rotated forward. Use the "QUIZ" to determine your tightest side. You only do this exercise on the tightest side. Do not switch to the other side to balance yourself. We are actually creating balance by only doing this exercise on the side that is out of balance. If you don't know what side is tightest, then skip this exercise.

On the Back

Realign the pelvis on your back

Lie down on your back and bring both knees up towards your chest so both feet are off the ground. Place your hand behind the knee of the side that is tightest (determined with the "QUIZ"). Squeeze your hand with your calf by bending your knee. At the same time, push against your hand, without moving, as if you're pushing your foot down towards the ground. Your hand will be resisting the pressure of your leg pressing against you. You don't need to press your hardest; a mild to moderate amount of pressure is just fine. The other leg is just up off the ground and not doing anything. It's important to keep it up off the ground so that it doesn't accidentally push into the ground or cheat in some way. There is no motion with this exercise, just pushing.

Push against your hand so that your foot is trying to touch the ground but not moving. Hold the push for two seconds, or one deep breath, and then relax. Repeat this push ten times. After those ten repetitions, your pelvis should be in better alignment.

In Standing

Realign the pelvis while standing

The side that is tight will be taking a step forward, relative to your other leg. In a standing position, push down into the ground with both feet and, using the friction of the ground, pull the feet towards each other without moving them. For example, if it's your right side that is the tightest iliacus, your right leg will have stepped forward, and, like scissors, your right leg will try to push backward while your left leg will try to move forward. There is no motion with this exercise, just pushing.

Hold the push for two seconds, or one deep breath, and then relax. Repeat this push ten times. After those ten repetitions, your pelvis should be in better alignment. This version is not as good as lying down, but if you're standing in line or at a concert it's a great way to realign your pelvis and help relax the iliacus.

In Sitting

Realign the pelvis while sitting

In sitting, take the leg of the side that is tightest, lift it off the ground, and wrap your hand behind that knee. For example, if your right iliacus is the tightest, you would put your hands behind your right thigh near your knee. Push down, without moving, against your hand as if you're going to put your foot back down on the floor. At the same time, you're going to be lifting the opposite leg up off the ground, like marching, against your arm. In this example, your right leg would be pushing against your hand, towards the ground, and your left leg is pushing up off the ground towards a marching position against your arm.

Hold the push for two seconds, or one deep breath, and then relax. Repeat this push ten times. After those ten repetitions, your pelvis should be in better alignment. This version is not as good as lying down, but if you're at the computer, dinner, or a meeting, it's a great way to realign your pelvis and help relax the iliacus.

Keep the Iliacus Relaxed

Now that you know how to get the iliacus to relax and the pelvis back in alignment, let's try to prevent it from getting tight again! The reality is, the lives we live offer a plentitude of opportunities to cause the iliacus to tighten again. Remember all those reasons in the section "Why Is My Hip So Tight?" Practically, you may not be able to completely eliminate all the reasons why the tight iliacus has developed in the first place, but every little effort you make will create a cumulative and positive effect. What is best is to know how to release it when it gets tight and manage your lifestyle to keep that muscle as healthy as possible. Once you put in the work to release it and see how great that area and the rest of the body feels you won't want that tightness to return.

Heat it up

In the beginning of the book, "Warm it up, Buttercup," we discussed how heat can help with tight and knotted muscles by increasing the blood flow to the area. Heat opens the blood vessels so the blood can really flow, bringing in nutrients for the muscle to heal and taking away toxins and minerals that are keeping it contracted and unhealthy. Effective sources of heat can be applied to the front and back of the hip to help these muscles to soften. Some examples of heat sources include a hot pack, sauna, hot tub, bath or shower, therapeutic laser, ultrasound, biomat, and other forms of light. Increasing circulation to the area is a simple tool that works fairly well in addition to other techniques for muscle knots and tension.

Figure 4 Stretch

A Figure 4 stretch lengthens muscles in the back of the hip, such as the piriformis muscle. Bringing circulation to this area of the body and releasing tension in the piriformis helps the iliacus because it keeps the Villains from tugging against it. Releasing tension in this area also helps to reduce pressure on the sciatic nerve, which can get pressed upon when the piriformis is tight.

Figure 4 stretch for the hip rotators with hands or using the wall

Lie on your back and cross one leg over the other so that your ankle is resting on your opposite knee. At this point, you have two options: one is to bring your hands behind your opposite knee and bring your knee up towards your chest until you feel a stretch. Alternatively, you can place that same foot on the wall. Both methods are effective; however, putting your foot up on the wall can also help facilitate relaxation because you're not having to strain the upper body by pulling with your hand. You should feel a stretch in the back of the hip and leg. If you feel any groin or knee pain, stop.

With this stretch you want to change the behavior of the muscle, different than just warming up a muscle. Therefore, hold this stretch for longer than normal, three to five minutes on each side. If you stop feeling the stretch either pull a little bit further or stop. It's not working if you don't feel it in the right place. One repetition per day is all that is needed.

Doing this on both sides is ideal. Don't forget to realign the pelvis after doing all of your stretches and exercises.

Crossover Stretch

This motion helps to stretch out the back of the hip, similar to the Figure 4 stretch, with a slightly different twist. Similarly, it mellows the tight glutes and hip rotator muscles that play tug-of-war with the iliacus.

Crossover stretch for the hip and lower back—stop if it
pinches in the front of the hip

Lie on your back, bring your arm out to a "T," and raise one leg up to the ceiling. The other leg is flat on the ground. Let the lifted leg cross over your body towards the floor.

With this stretch you want to change the behavior of the muscle, different than just warming up a muscle. Therefore, hold this stretch for longer than normal, three to five minutes on each side. If you stop feeling the stretch either pull a little bit further or stop. *Caution:* If you notice any pinching in your hip or groin with this motion, stop. You should feel a nice, gentle sensation in the back of your hip near your glute, and maybe even your lower back. It's not working if you don't feel it in the right place. One repetition per day is all that is needed.

Doing this on both sides is ideal. Don't forget to realign the pelvis after doing all of your stretches and exercises.

Lunge Stretch

A lunge actually stretches the iliopsoas, bringing circulation and length to that muscle. Step one foot forward with your spine straight. You can do this stretch with your knee on or off the ground. With this stretch, it's important to engage your abdominal muscles or contract your glutes to eliminate the forward tilt of the pelvis and tuck your butt under you. This allows for the iliopsoas muscle to stretch fully over the joint. It also helps to protect the lower back from the psoas tugging on it while it's being stretched. You should feel the stretch in the front of your hip joint or the front of your thigh. If you're not feeling it there or you are feeling it in a different spot, then stop. You can experiment with bending your spine to the opposite side of the leg you're stretching to increase the stretch of the psoas.

The lunge stretch for the iliopsoas works best when the pelvis is tucked underneath you. Experiment with bending your trunk to the side to involve the psoas in the stretch even more.

With this stretch you want to change the behavior of the muscle, different than just warming up a muscle. Therefore, hold this stretch for longer than normal, three to five minutes on each side. If you stop feeling the stretch either pull a little bit further or stop. You should not feel it in your back, tailbone, or glute. It's not working if you don't feel it in the right place. One repetition per day is all that is needed.

Doing this on both sides is ideal. Don't forget to realign the pelvis after doing all of your stretches and exercises.

Clamshell

Strengthening the side of your hip, the gluteus medius, is a great way to support the hip and pelvis, reducing the workload of the iliopsoas. This exercise is surprisingly challenging but vital to the health of the hips. The clamshell exercise has been found to be the most effective exercise to isolate and strengthen this muscle (Barton et al., 2018; Boren et al., 2011).

Lie on your side with both knees bent and your feet together. Lift your knees apart, keeping your top knee right above your bottom knee and your feet touching each other. The tendency with this exercise is to let the top knee sway in an arch toward the back of the body and not stay right over the bottom knee. When that happens, the correct muscles are not getting strengthened. In order to keep the top knee directly above the bottom knee, it's useful to think about pushing that top knee not only up but a little bit forward.

Doing this correctly, you won't be able to lift your knee very high, and, in fact, you'll get tired pretty quickly. The goal would be to do twenty repetitions of this exercise nice and slow and controlled on the way up and on the way down.

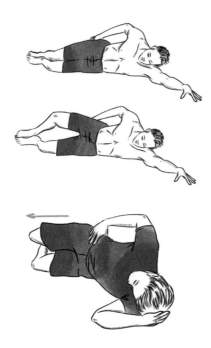

Clamshell exercise to strengthen the gluteus medius—make sure to keep that top knee directly over the bottom one

Doing this on both sides is ideal. Don't forget to realign the pelvis after doing all of your stretches and exercises.

Core Strength

The iliacus and psoas don't have to work so hard when other muscles around the spine and hips do their part to keep the core strong. Good core stability involves strong abdominal, hip, and back muscles and coordination of those muscles so they work together with the iliopsoas to hold this area stable.

There are many different exercises and methods for strengthening the core; there is a plethora of resources on the subject. Seek a personal trainer, physical therapist, or other movement professional to guide you. When choosing core exercises, choose the ones that don't primarily use the iliopsoas muscles themselves. See "Careful with Iliopsoas Strengthening and Pilates" for some examples of these kinds of exercises to avoid.

An important area to strengthen in the core is the transverse abdominis, the deepest layer of the abdominal muscles. This muscle is responsible for giving the spine space to move. It wraps around the abdomen and acts like a balloon. If you were to squeeze a balloon from the sides, the balloon gets taller from top to bottom. Similarly, when the transverse abdominis is strong and contracted, it takes the pressure off and gives the lower spine space. That added support to the spine helps the psoas and the iliacus not have to work so hard.

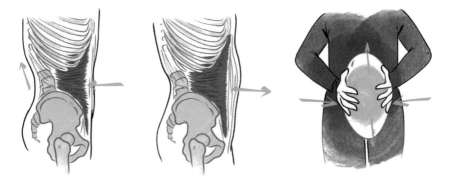

The transverse abdominis acts like a balloon by squeezing in on the abdomen, creating more space and support for the spine

The transverse abdominis is an endurance muscle, meaning to do its job, it needs to be able to hold a contraction for a long time. That's why exercises like a plank, where you are holding it for as long as you can, help to train the muscle for the job at hand. You can plank on your knees or toes and elbows or hands. Hold the plank of your choice, keeping your spine straight, for as long as you can. Then rest and repeat three times, each time holding it as long as you can. You should feel it work your arms and shoulder blades and your stomach. If it hurts your back, try to lift your abdomen up a little bit or stop.

Different ways to do a plank exercise to strengthen the transverse abdominis

Fist Squeeze

This exercise helps your pelvis to align itself at the pubic bone. This is an add-on exercise to the pelvic realignment exercise to help get everything back in place and is best done immediately after the realignment exercise.

Fist squeeze to help align the pubic bone

Lie on your back, bend your knees, and put both your feet flat on the floor. Put your fists in between your knees and squeeze your fists with both of your knees for a count of five. Release and repeat five times. You may feel or hear a pop from your pelvis and that's totally normal. That's just your pelvis aligning itself.

Breathe

We are surrounded by a multitude of stressful situations every day. As we are all aware, this stress affects our mind, muscles, nerves, immune system, and nearly every other organ in the body. There are two ways to mitigate the effects of stress. One is to decrease the cause: remove yourself from stressful situations, say "no" to adding more to your plate, or consider a job change.

The other side of the coin is to manage the stress you have. There are a lot of causes of stress in our lives that we frankly can't change. But you can take a walk outside, breathe in fresh air, or watch a funny movie to reduce the effect of stress on your body. Try a breathing technique, yoga, meditation, mindfulness practice, a cuddle with a pet, or a warm Epsom salt bath, whatever works for you. The point is, a stress-lessening technique or two should be a daily practice given the crazy world we live in, just as important as brushing your teeth every day.

Breathing is a simple form of stress reduction that significantly affects whether the iliopsoas stays tight. As you take deep breaths into your abdomen, it allows for your body to regain a sense of balance. It allows for the flight or fight, the stress response, to diminish. Breathing has a special effect on the iliopsoas because of the connection of the psoas to the diaphragm. The connective tissue of the diaphragm blends with the psoas which blends with the iliacus, making one complete "C" shape.

Even taking just three deep breaths can change the way the nervous system works. Stress is a major reason for tight muscles, including the iliopsoas. It's hard for muscles to relax under a threatening situation, and deep breaths into the abdomen is a simple way to lessen the threat.

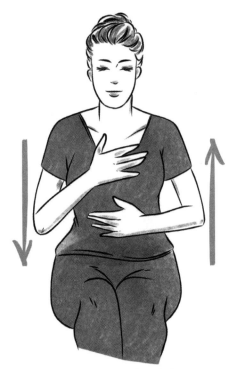

Take three deep breaths every hour into the abdomen using your hands as a guide to make sure the breath comes from the abdomen and not the chest

Set your timer for once every hour. When your timer goes off, it's time for that deep breath. Take that moment to close your eyes and take three deep breaths into your abdomen. Have one hand on your stomach and one on your chest to make sure your stomach is moving as you breathe and not your chest. This will help to keep your stress response in check and your hips relaxed.

Align the Spine

If the rest of the spine is aligned, it makes it easier for the iliacus and psoas to hold the spine and pelvis in place. Even aligning the bones in the upper neck can make an impact on the alignment of the hips. Working with a professional like a chiropractor, osteopath, or physical therapist who is trained in techniques to align the spine can make a difference. A healthy spine means a healthy nervous system. The brain, spinal cord, and nerves control not only pain, sensation, and movement, but all of our body's internal functions as well, including the stress response. An aligned spine is an important part of the health of the body as a whole and the hip and pelvic region as well.

Release Neighboring Tight Spots

Many of the Villain and Sidekick muscles related to the iliacus can also get tight and develop trigger points in response to a tight iliacus. They are going to need some attention as well. Trigger points are a special kind of knot in the muscle that, when "triggered," creates pain somewhere else, as mentioned in "Knots and Triggers."

These diagrams highlight the muscles that are commonly tight when the iliopsoas is tight. The X on the diagram shows where the trigger point is located. When that X is pressed, the sensation will refer to somewhere in the shaded area. Remember, trigger points can be latent or active. The active ones will refer pain even when they are not pressed upon; the latent ones need pressure on the X for the pain to be created. If you are having pain in any of these referral areas, it could be caused by a trigger point.

To address one of these trigger points, make sure the tension in the primary muscles in "Step 1" and "Step 2" have been released first. Then, using these images as a guide, place prolonged pressure on these points for thirty to ninety seconds, whatever it takes for the soreness to lessen or disappear.

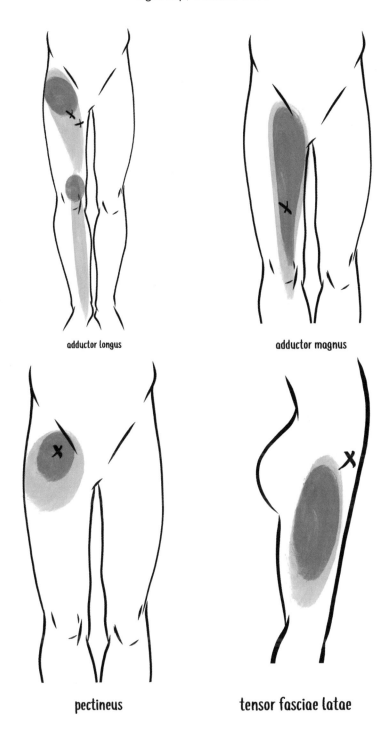

adductor longus

adductor magnus

pectineus

tensor fasciae latae

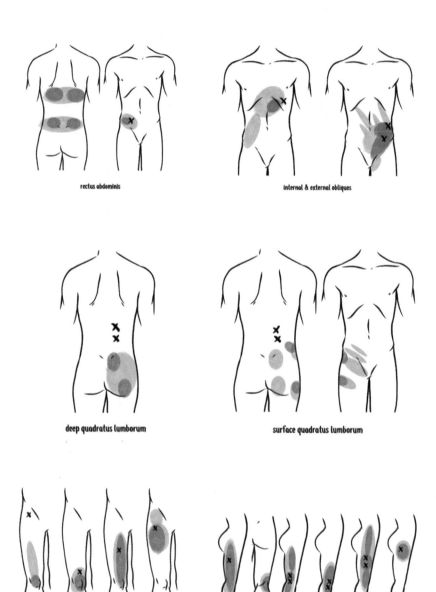

rectus abdominis

internal & external obliques

deep quadratus lumborum

surface quadratus lumborum

quadricep

quadricep

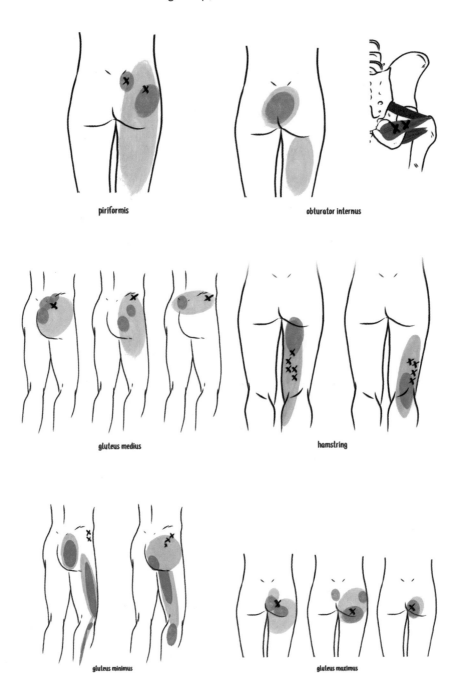

piriformis

obturator internus

gluteus medius

hamstring

gluteus minimus

gluteus maximus

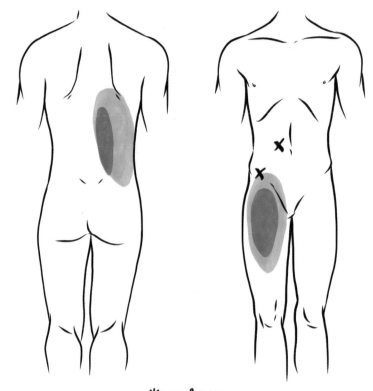

iliacus & psoas

Trigger points of the hip and core region—use these drawings as a guide for finding trigger points in the muscles, marked as an X, that could be causing pain in the shaded areas (*Travell, Simons, & Simons*)

One of the most common muscles tight alongside the iliacus is the TFL (tensor fasciae latae). The TFL then pulls on the IT band and irritates the outside of the hip down to the knee. We discussed in "You Are Not on a Roll" how rolling the IT band is treating the symptom and not the cause and is not good for your IT band. Using a racquetball-size tool to put prolonged pressure on this muscle works great. The TFL is on the outside of the pelvic bone, right around the corner from the iliacus. Use your fingers, a ball, or tool to apply the pressure to the TFL. Hold the prolonged pressure for thirty to ninety seconds, whatever it takes for the soreness to lessen or disappear.

Releasing the TFL with a ball will help keep the iliacus relaxed. A tight TFL contributes to IT band issues. The IT band is not meant to be massaged or rolled; treat the TFL instead.

141

Another commonly tight and undertreated muscle that plays tug-of-war with the iliacus is the obturator internus. This muscle has a major role of holding the hip joint together, acting like a mirror to the iliacus. Because of its location, being hidden around the corner like the iliacus, it too is undertreated yet often responsible for pain around the hip, sciatic nerve, and pelvic floor.

This muscle is best released internally by a practitioner through the vagina or the rectum. From the outside of the body, you can release this muscle by sitting on your fingertips with your palm facing up. Curl the fingertips around the inside surface of the sit bone like a "C" and apply that prolonged pressure to those tender spots. Hold the prolonged pressure for thirty to ninety seconds, whatever it takes for the soreness to lessen or disappear.

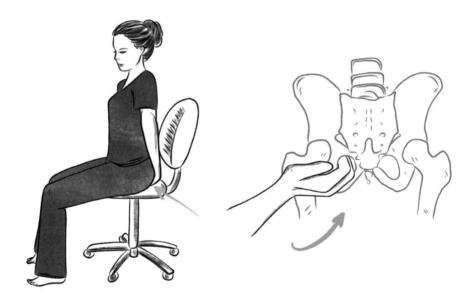

Self obturator internus release by sitting on your hand and curling your fingers to the inside surface of the sit bone

You only need to do a trigger point release once a day or even once every other day. Make sure you read the above introduction in "3 Simple Steps" so you know how much pressure to use and what you should feel.

Shoes

Proper shoe wear can make a big difference in whether you have a tight iliopsoas. People who wear high heels, up on their toes, create a forward tilt of the pelvis. Remember, the iliacus also pulls the pelvis forward, so wearing heels just increases that tendency and helps the iliacus stay tight. Wearing flat shoes helps the iliacus relax.

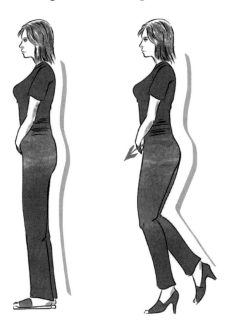

Wearing heels contributes to an anteriorly rotated pelvis and tight iliopsoas

Good arch supports in your shoes helps the iliacus get back on track as well. There are many shoes in the market with a good arch (see "Resources"). If you tend to have tightness in your iliopsoas on one side, your pelvis is going to be rotated forward on that side and that foot ends up being flatter (overpronated). By releasing the tension in the iliacus and glute, as well as aligning the pelvis, the foot doesn't get pushed into being flat.

This issue can be addressed from both ends of the train: at the pelvis and at the foot. If, at the same time you are implementing the "3 Simple Steps" to release your iliacus and align your pelvis, you can wear shoes that are supporting the arch and preventing that arch from falling flat,

143

you're helping to solidify the correct pelvic alignment. Shoe wear that helps keep the arch of the foot supported not only helps the pelvis stay level but also supports the feet, knees, hips, and spine. This is especially important for those with flexible feet and overly flexible bodies that often need more support than average. Good shoe wear, a relaxed iliacus, and an aligned pelvis address the issue at both ends of the chain.

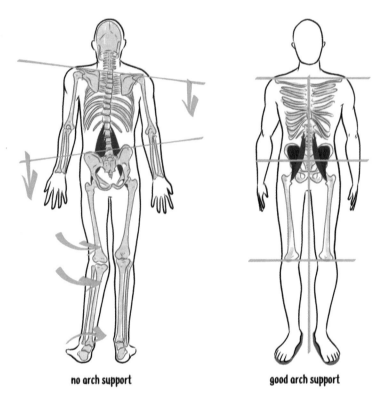

no arch support   good arch support

Good arch support can help support a rotated pelvis from the ground up

Orthotics

Similar to good arch supports in shoes, orthotics can help keep the iliacus relaxed and the pelvis aligned. Orthotics can be made by a podiatrist, physical therapist, chiropractor, and many other health professionals. Some can even be purchased over-the-counter. Having a custom-made orthotic that you can put in the shoes that you already have is a great alternative to buying new shoes with good arches. Plus, it's tailored to your foot to make sure that it's giving you the proper support that you need. By wearing orthotics and proper shoe wear you are supporting proper alignment of your pelvis, helping the iliacus to stay relaxed.

Limit Driving and Sitting

Limiting the amount of sitting and driving can have a significant impact on whether you have a tight iliopsoas. If you're doing the work to release your iliopsoas and align your pelvis, it makes sense to reduce the impact of what caused the tightness to begin with. Decreasing the amount of sitting and driving is a tall task, especially when we have duties with our job and family that require this of us. Stand-up desks and the many related accessories are becoming popular for this reason.

Whether you have a standing desk or not, movement is key, so creating breaks in the day to change position is ideal. Every thirty minutes you can set an alarm to go off that reminds you to "stand up." Don't waste time, just stand up, walk around, move your spine from side to side, do a lunge stretch or a realignment exercise, and then go back to your work. Don't make it complicated. It really only takes a fifteen-second break to give that iliopsoas muscle a break from having to hold you up in sitting all day long.

Similarly, take a break every hour or two during those long road trips. Get out, do a few stretches and the pelvic realignment exercise, and then get back on the road. This makes a huge difference in the health of your iliacus and the rest of your body.

Eliminating sitting is not an option for most of us. However, knowing how to mitigate the effects of sitting and how to release the iliacus and align the pelvis gives you the tools to manage the effect that sitting has on your body.

Sitting Tips

Standing or treadmill desks are becoming mainstream and do wonders for our sitting culture. Many of these desks allow for both standing and sitting, giving your body a break from one position. Standing or sitting all day isn't great for your body; movement and changing positions is best. Change your position by stretching during a phone call or walking for a meeting. Take a quick walk around the office or grab a deep breath from outdoors.

If you haven't quite implemented a standing desk strategy, or still need to figure out how to sit in a healthy way at the board meeting or out to dinner with friends, here are some tips. Our tendency is to either slouch or sit with our back arched too much. It's ideal to find that middle ground where we're not totally slouching, but we're not completely arching the back. In that neutral position, the iliopsoas doesn't have to work as hard. The best way to do this is to imagine being pulled up to the sky by a string attached to your sternum right between your breasts. Be tall when you're sitting.

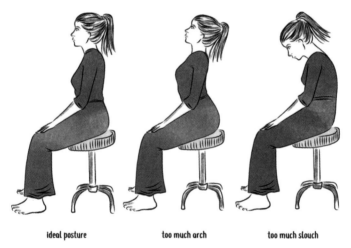

ideal posture   too much arch   too much slouch

The ideal posture for the lower back and the hips is a neutral position, not too far arched or slouched

You can position yourself in a way to take the strain off of the iliopsoas muscle by adjusting your seat to be slightly higher than your knees. Sometimes it's useful to have a firm pillow or a slanted wedge on your chair that's pointing downward to the front of the chair so that your hips are above your knees and your pelvis is on an incline. This will make it so that your iliopsoas doesn't have to work so hard to hold you upright, and it will create a little more space in the hip joint.

Sitting for a happy iliopsoas

Another strategy is to take the side with the tightest iliacus (see "QUIZ") and put that foot underneath the chair. By doing this, it creates that added space in the hip joint, allowing the iliopsoas and the hip joint to have space and not get squished. Another easy way to get the knees below the hips is using a kneeling chair. Kneeling chairs similarly open up the hip joint and create less tension on the iliopsoas.

Sitting on a therapy ball is a great way to engage your muscles during sitting but it can be too much for an iliopsoas that is unhappy. That muscle already has to work hard to hold you upright. Add in an unstable surface and that muscle works overtime, increasing the chance that it will decide to be tight for good.

While sitting cross-legged, as in meditation, it's useful to put blocks under your knees and to have something that you're sitting upon. There are some great meditation cushions on the market that help the pelvis to be in good alignment so that you're not having to engage the iliopsoas to hold you up so much. A cushion that slants downward towards the front is ideal (see "Resources"). Other positions such as kneeling with your bottom on a couple of blocks or a cushion helps to open up the space where the iliopsoas lives. Rolling up a blanket or towel under your ankles puts your feet in a happy place.

Meditation postures for a happy iliopsoas

Driving Tips

As I mentioned, taking breaks during your road trip is essential. If you can get out of the car every hour or two, stretch and align the pelvis—it'll make a huge difference in the health of your iliacus. In fact, stretching and realigning the pelvis is a great thing to do quickly every single time you get out of the car; it doesn't take more than thirty seconds.

When driving, the right leg is used to manipulate the pedals, and therefore there is a constant contraction of the iliopsoas while driving. Using cruise control when applicable makes a huge difference. When you do use cruise control, try to let your leg relax, and maybe even turn your knee outwards slightly when it's not having to work the pedals. If possible, position the seat so that the hips are as high as they can be over the knees. Low-riding cars make this nearly impossible.

Driving posture for a happy iliopsoas—hips above the knees, elbows by side, right leg resting out to the side

Be mindful of how much tension you're holding in that hip as you're driving. Overuse of the iliopsoas is pretty unavoidable when driving; after all, the right iliopsoas is constantly holding the right leg in a ready position to accelerate or brake. Add in a clutch and the left side gets to work overtime too. Driving can be quite a challenge for the iliopsoas. Consider carpooling or taking public transportation when you can.

More Strength, Less Stretch if Too Bendy

If you're already very flexible you may want to consider limiting the amount of stretching you do. More isn't always better. A great example of this happens often in yoga. As the yogi continues to practice and become more flexible, the stretches get deeper and deeper with various poses. But there is a limit to how much your body is supposed to stretch. In order for the body to work at its best, there needs to be a balance of flexibility and stability. If you are too flexible, that balance is off.

Continuing to improve flexibility, the body gets to a point where it is no longer stretching muscles—it is stretching ligaments and joint capsules. These structures aren't supposed to be stretched. If you tend to be someone who is really flexible and can, for example, easily go over into a forward fold and put your hands flat on the ground, or rest your stomach on your thighs in long sitting, that is plenty of flexibility. Similarly, you don't need more flexibility if you can go into the splits or lay all the way down in a pigeon pose. All these examples are *way* past what is needed for a healthy amount of flexibility. You will end up making the muscles tighten up around the joints to stabilize you or pinching and straining the joint itself.

The iliacus and psoas will stay more relaxed if they don't have to do all the work to keep you held together. Focusing on strengthening activities that involve motion towards the center is a great way to give those muscles some help in stabilizing the back, hip, and pelvis. During yoga, for example, in a Warrior II pose, the stance can be shortened and the focus becomes pushing down into the ground and pulling the legs towards each other, without moving, instead of going deeper into the pose. Exercises that strengthen the core and the hip, such as Barre classes and core stability methods, can also be really useful at helping to stabilize unstable hips. When the hips become more stable, the iliopsoas muscle is going to be less likely to knot up to try to hold you together.

Focus on strength and pulling to the center in yoga instead of deeper poses

Careful with Yoga

Yoga is full of opportunities for aggravating the iliopsoas and twisting the pelvis out of alignment. The biggest thing that causes tightness of the iliopsoas in yoga is stretching beyond what the body is built to do. Once you have achieved a certain level of flexibility that's functional, pushing yourself further and further into acrobatic experiences may seem desirable but it can be harmful. It creates more instability, which will make it more likely for the iliopsoas to hold on to stabilize that too loose hip and pelvis region. I'm not saying to stop doing yoga. As with any activity, it's important to know the risks and to make an educated decision before embarking on deeper yoga poses.

Because there's so much focus on the hip joint in yoga, with "hip openers" being a class favorite, the hip is an area that is commonly overstretched and too loose. The words "hip opener" should be outlawed because it really encourages people to continue to open and overstretch the hip joint when this joint is meant to be strong and stable. Asking yourself, "Is the human body designed to do that?" before taking on a pose is essential. The best kept secret in yoga is famous yoga teachers escaping to India to get hip replacement surgeries.

Stop stretching deeper when you've achieved a baseline level of flexibility. For example, with the hamstring, a normal level of flexibility is lying on your back and having your hamstring stop your leg when it is perpendicular to the floor. Anything beyond that is excess. Look around any yoga class full of forward folds with palms to the ground and you will see firsthand a room full of tight iliacus muscles, trying to stabilize over-flexible hips.

Second, any type of activity where one leg is going forward and the other leg is going backward is going to have a high probability of pulling your pelvis out of alignment and causing that iliopsoas to tighten up. Many of the standing poses—Warrior I, Warrior II, side angle pose, triangle pose—have a tendency to rotate the pelvis because one leg is forward and the other one is back, twisting the hips. This is precarious for the pelvis and the iliopsoas, especially when you push deeper into the pose.

Normal hamstring flexibility, anything more is excessive

This doesn't mean you have to stop doing these poses altogether. All the poses can be done in a way where your legs are closer together and the focus is more on the strengthening, posture, focus, and breathing instead. Ginger Garner, PT, author of *Medical Therapeutic Yoga*, is a pioneer in the field of hip-safe yoga. Her material is full of specific tweaks for keeping this area of the body healthy and prolonging your yoga practice throughout your lifetime without injury. Simple changes to your yoga practice, such as pigeon on your back versus full pigeon, will go a long way to keeping your pelvis aligned and your iliacus happy.

Do pigeon on your back and not full pigeon, for example, to limit postures where one leg is forward and the other is back, creating a pelvic rotation

Shorten stance on Warrior and lunge poses

Using the principles of decreasing the distance between your feet in a lunge-like pose, not bringing one leg forward and the other back to the extreme, and monitoring how deep you're going into a pose will keep you practicing yoga into your wisest years by preventing you from injuring your hips. Try pushing down and in with the legs in a lunge-type pose, limit overactivity of the iliopsoas in poses like staff or standing hand to toe, and view progression in yoga as getting stronger and more at peace in the pose versus deeper.

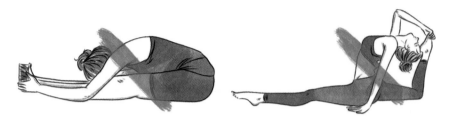

Avoid overstretching the hip and spine

Warrior II with shortened stance and pushing down
and in with elongated spine

Avoid working the iliopsoas too much

Tightness is a Good Thing

The brain creates tightness for a reason. Sometimes it's related to trauma or surgery that has long passed and isn't applicable anymore. Sometimes it's as a result of an unstable or injured area that is still a problem in the present moment. For example, someone with an unstable hip joint due to the bones they were born with will always have some sort of signal from the brain asking the iliacus and psoas to work extra hard to hold it all together. If indeed your body does need the stability that your muscles are providing, releasing the tension may not be a good thing. However, leaving that tightness to run wild will only create an opportunity for something along the chain to get aggravated or worn down. What should we do in this catch-22?

The tension in the iliacus muscle, if left to its own devices, will create problems; it should be released from time to time. The frequency of the muscle releases can be less and the focus should be on methods of stabilizing and strengthening the hip and spine areas. For those of us who are unstable, strengthening becomes a larger than average focus of our wellness routine. With strong muscles around the hip and spine, the iliacus and psoas still have to help stabilize, but not in a way that makes them as tight.

Careful with Iliopsoas Strengthening and Pilates

Exercises that use the hip flexors a lot are *not* the kinds of exercises that will be useful when you have a tight iliopsoas. Muscles that are tight do not want to be strengthened. They have been contracted for possibly years on end and they do not want to be asked to work more. What they need is to relax and for the brain to tell them that it's OK to release their tension. When you use a muscle that already has tension in it, it's like asking a tight rubber band to contract more. By contracting the taut muscle, it pulls even more on the pelvis and spine, increasing the likelihood of rotating the pelvis even more.

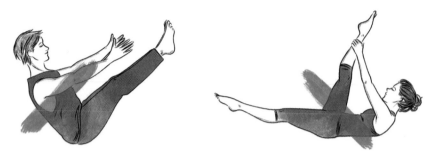

Examples of exercises that overwork an already tired iliopsoas

Activities that involve a lot of hip flexion, moving the leg forward or lifting the leg up, are the exercises to be really cautious about. We mentioned this in "Careful with Yoga" as well. There are quite a few exercises in yoga and Pilates that use the iliopsoas, so ask your instructor to help you modify those if you have issues with this muscle. Other types of exercises that use the iliopsoas quite a bit include a full sit-up, boat pose, marching exercises, step classes, and step machines. It's important to limit these types of exercises if you already have a tight and sensitive iliacus.

Careful with Deep Lunges

Caution should be taken when doing deep lunges when you have issues with a tight iliopsoas. Deep lunges put one foot forward in relation to the foot that's behind and sets you up for the possibility of facilitating a pelvic rotation. If your pelvis is on the verge of rotating because your iliopsoas is a little tight, lunging might push it over the edge. Avoiding deep lunges and instead doing strengthening exercises that utilize both of your legs symmetrically, like a squat, is best for your healing iliacus.

Avoid deep lunges, do box squats instead

Careful with Deep Squats

Deep squats put the hip and the iliopsoas into a shortened position while making the iliopsoas have to work very hard to stabilize the hip and spine. The heavier the weight, the more work that shortened muscle has to do to stabilize you. A deep squat is where your hips go below the level of your knees, hips close to the heels.

Avoid deep squats, do box squats instead

157

A chair squat, or a box squat, is a great, iliacus-safe alternative. This is where your hip stops at the level of your knees, and your hips and knees are closer to 90 degrees. This is much safer for the iliopsoas as it will not create such a cramped space for the muscle while it's being asked to work so hard.

Move

Any kind of movement reverses the effects of tightness. Not only does movement increase circulation throughout all the muscles of the body, but it also inhibits the brain's creation of pain. Just taking a short twenty-minute walk after work, parking further away from the entrance, or taking the stairs goes a long way to decreasing muscle tightness and pain, not to mention the benefit to the heart, lungs, and metabolism. Find some sort of movement you can do each day to help keep the body from being tight and sore.

Calm Inflammation

Decreasing the overall inflammation in your body will help your body deal and heal from any type of injury, including injuries related to the iliopsoas. Your body is constantly creating inflammation as your body tries to heal and keep itself healthy. Inflammation is also created as part of our immune system that fights infections. Inflammation is actually a good thing.

Inflammation becomes a bad thing when there is too much and the body can't handle it. The body continues to make inflammation in response to injuries, disease processes, infection fighting, stress, food, and the environment. This inflammation accumulates in the body and, just like a teacup, continues to get more and more full. When the body can keep up with the inflammatory process, the teacup fills a little and then empties. Over time the level of inflammation in the teacup is rising and falling, rising and falling. When there's too much inflammation created and the body cannot manage it, the teacup overflows. That's when we experience symptoms related to inflammation.

The plethora of causes of inflammation can quickly overflow the teacup and manifest in symptoms. You could have, for example, a tight iliopsoas and an issue with your pelvic alignment and have only mild symptoms if your teacup hasn't overflowed. But if your cup is overflowing and you have a lot of inflammation in your body, something that's very minor, like a slightly tight iliacus, can cause a lot of pain. Addressing your inflammatory load is key to the healing process. There are great books on anti-inflammatory diets, so you can learn what to eat and what to avoid to help you manage your inflammation. In my experience, nutritionists, naturopathic doctors, and functional medicine doctors are experts in addressing inflammation in the body and supporting the healing process with foods and natural means (See "Resources").

Frequency Specific Microcurrent

FSM (Frequency Specific Microcurrent) was first used in 1996 to treat trigger points and is one of the most effective tools to date. It is a subtle treatment due to its low-level electrical stimulation that is below what you can feel, producing not so subtle results. A frequency is how many beats per minute that the current enters the body. Specific frequencies are chosen to seemingly change the way the muscle and the brain are behaving, allowing for these holding patterns and swampy muscles to become supple once again.

In the most recent edition of the iconic *Myofascial Pain and Dysfunction: The Trigger Point Manual*, FSM is listed amongst the handful of effective tools to treat trigger points. In my experience it deserves high ranking. Just like an opera singer can hit a note that shatters crystal, so can a frequency of the microcurrent create a biological resonance that assists the body in its healing. FSM also increases the energy production of the cells by 500 percent while it's being delivered (Seegers et al., 2001), presumably giving the muscle the energy to relax. Studies have also shown its anti-inflammatory effects as well, decreasing inflammatory markers by ten to twenty times in only ninety minutes (McMakin et al., 2005).

Many FSM treatment sequences have been developed specifically for trigger points. Trigger points caused by head and neck trauma are treated differently than those related to the iliopsoas, discs, and spinal joints. With the most common side effect as euphoria and many stories of effectiveness, FSM is a no-brainer tool to implement. This treatment needs to be delivered by a trained practitioner who can make sure that it is safe for you. You can find those trained in this method on the FSM site in the "References" section.

Class IV Laser

For years the use of Class IV therapeutic laser has been a go-to tool for not only releasing tension in the muscle, but also for helping to heal the irritated structure affected by the tight iliacus muscle. As mentioned in "Knots and Triggers," tight muscles benefit from heat and increased circulation, and this type of laser does the trick.

Class IV laser is a much higher intensity of infrared light than a cold laser, resulting in not only the healing benefits of the light itself, but also the deep warmth that it provides. The higher powered the laser, the more it can deliver its benefits to deeper targets in a shorter amount of time. Most Class IV lasers are thirty to sixty times more powerful than a cold laser. In comparison to other forms of heating treatments, this kind of laser can increase heat of the tissue up to two inches deep, compared to ultrasound at up to one inch deep and a heating pad only one-half inch deep. This allows for a Class IV laser to get to those deep muscles in the glute and the iliopsoas muscle.

Laser not only increases circulation, taking away toxins in the muscle and providing fresh nutrients and oxygen, but it also speeds up the production of energy to the cells, helping them to do their work. Cells like the macrophage cells (the parts of our immune system that clean up broken tissue and debris) become more active, cleaning up the area and helping the body to heal. This optimal healing environment decreases inflammation, swelling, muscle tightness, stiffness, and pain while improving the body's ability to heal itself. Plus it feels amazing. This treatment is delivered by a licenced practitioner for safety. Lasers of this intensity are very powerful.

Dry Needling and Trigger Point Injections

Although having a needle placed into your muscle does not sound like an appealing proposition, trigger point needling is a very effective tool for those spots that just won't let go. Wet needling refers to injecting a substance into the muscle whereas dry needling involves a technique using small acupuncture-sized needles with nothing injected. Both have been found to be effective (Travell, Simons, & Simons).

Dry needling is less invasive and has become a popular method delivered by physical therapists in some states as well as acupuncturists and other providers. This technique targets the trigger point and attempts to change its activated state, helping the muscle to regain its soft and supple function. If an unaddressed tight iliacus lurks beneath the surface while other trigger points are targeted with a needling method, the effects of the treatment may be temporary. Addressing the tight iliacus through pressure release or needling, along with treating other muscles, allows for the best possible outcome. Seek a practitioner who is well trained in this method to ensure that the needles are placed correctly and safely.

Brace Yourself

Braces that wrap around the SI (sacroiliac) joints can help keep the pelvis in alignment when your tailbone is very irritated and needs some extra support as it heals. These are most useful with an unstable pelvis and an aggressively tight iliacus that is causing pain around the tailbone or SI joints (see "Resources").

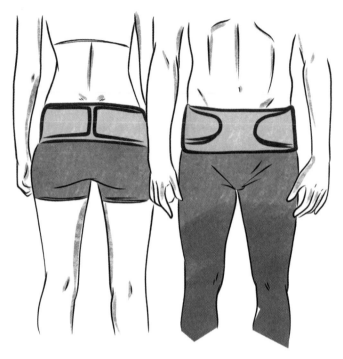

Sacroiliac (SI) brace

Any kind of brace should be used as a temporary tool to help you get through a painful period. Ultimately the goal is for the iliacus muscle to relax, the pelvis to get in better alignment, and it to stay aligned on its own. The brace is something that is useful to help with symptoms temporarily but not something that you should wear indefinitely.

Tape

Kinesiotape is a great tool to help stabilize where the tailbone and the pelvic bones meet. This is useful for the time when you're working through the exercises and the initial healing process. There are many techniques for taping the body to support muscles and joints as they are healing and there are great resources for these techniques online, as well as many health practitioners with specialized training on tape application.

Sacroiliac (SI) kinesiology tape technique

Get Help

Everyone's body is different. If you're finding that part of this information is useful to you but you're still having symptoms, there may be a piece of the puzzle that is being missed. It's important to always consult the medical professionals that you trust before embarking on any new regimen or if you have unresolved symptoms.

There are many different professionals that can help you with a tight iliacus and a rotated pelvis, including physical therapists, chiropractors, trainers, and massage therapists—anyone who does body work and understands how the body is put together. Enrolling these professionals as part of your healing team is valuable to tweak the solutions in this book to your own individual situation.

Professionals like naturopathic doctors and nutritionists are also essential team members and can provide great insight into how you can decrease inflammation and speed healing through natural and safe methods. Furthermore, seeking counseling, energy work, and acupuncture can make a huge difference in your ability to recover from stress and trauma. Remember, you want to address all of the pieces of the puzzle for optimal results.

There are many different treatments that are not included in this book. Treatments that might help speed up the healing include other muscle and fascia work, manipulations to align the bones in the spine, hip, and pelvis, identification of various faulty movement patterns, and strengthening the core.

The focus of this book is on the impact of the iliacus and psoas muscles, and it is exciting to know that you just might have uncovered the hidden cause of your pain. Although a tight iliopsoas is a hugely undertreated issue, it is not the only cause. If the tools in this book do not resolve your pain, keep looking. There's likely another "why" that needs to be addressed too. Don't hesitate to consult your healthcare team to dig deeper.

CONCLUSION

Wow, the iliacus is an important muscle after all. It has finally come out of the closet and onto the main stage. Thank you for joining me on this journey of untwisting the core that has been bound up for way too long. You are now one of the few who have mastered the iliacus muscle amongst a sea of people oblivious to its nature. You can now talk about the iliacus at a cocktail party, how it's driving the alignment of the rest of the body, and why it's so tight.

Most importantly, you now know how you can care for your iliacus and your hips on your own. You can not only resolve the tightness that you have had for ages and then align the rotated pelvis that is contributing to your problem, but you can also prevent that tightness from happening in the future.

While we may not want to return to a time without chairs, hunting and gathering all day long, the future is here. Standing desks, self-driving cars, and the use of the Hip Hook will become the norm. The healing path has been laid; now all you need to do is follow the 3 Simple Steps.

As a special gift to my readers, I have compiled a series of videos of the releases and exercises discussed in the book as well as your very own *Tight Hip, Twisted Core* exercise handout. Access this gift at TightHipTwistedCore.com/ReadersGift.

The Iliacus Queen is just a mouse click away. Do reach out to me with any questions you may have. You can find me at christinekoth. com. I'd be honored to hear your honest book review on Amazon and would love to hear your iliacus story. It's been an honor to support you thus far and I look forward to walking by your side as you continue on your healing journey.

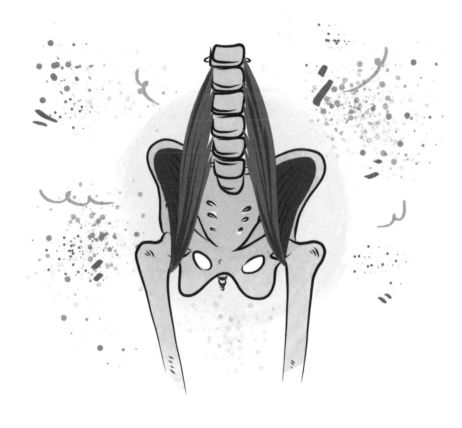

GLOSSARY

Beighton scale: a 9-point scale that measures for whole body joint hypermobility

Biomat: a mat made of crystals and light elements that produces a therapeutic and relaxation effect from infrared light

Bursitis: inflammation of a fluid-filled sac that is intended to protect an area of the body that needs extra protection

Core: the central part of the body that connects the upper and lower halves consisting of the abdomen, pelvis, and hips

Craniosacral therapy: a treatment technique that guides the bones in the skull to move smoothly so that spinal fluid can bathe the brain

Ileocecal valve: the valve that is the doorway between the small and large intestine

Iliacus: a muscle on the inside surface of the pelvis that connects the hip to the pelvis and helps to keep the pelvic bones in alignment

Iliopsoas: the combined name for both the iliacus and psoas muscles referred to together

Inguinal hernia: stretching of the abdominal wall near the groin that creates a pouch for intestine to enter it

Labrum: specialized and softer cartilage in the hip that helps to stabilize the hip and absorb force

Macrophage: a cell that the immune system uses to clean up broken tissue and debris in the body

Meniscus: specialized and softer cartilage in the knee that helps to stabilize the knee and absorb force

Myofascial release: a treatment technique that releases the adhesions in the tissue (fascia) that surrounds the muscles and organs with gentle pressure.

Psoas: a muscle deep in the abdomen that attaches to both the spine and the front of the hip and works to stabilize this region

Release: to cause a muscle that is tight and knotted to relax and become soft and supple

SI joint: the joint that connects the tailbone to the pelvis

Tendonitis: inflammation of the tendon, the structure that attaches a muscle to a bone

Tensor fasciae latae: a muscle on the outside of the hip that often gets tight alongside the iliacus

Trigger point: a type of muscle knot that, when pressed or activated, will produce pain somewhere else

Trigger point release: a treatment technique that provides prolonged pressure to a muscle to resolve the knot that is causing the trigger point to refer pain somewhere else

REFERENCES

Bishop, B.M., et al. "Electromyographic Analysis of Gluteus Maximus, Gluteus Medius, and Tensor Fascia Latae During Therapeutic Exercises with and without Elastic Resistance," *International Journal of Sports Physical Therapy* 13:4 (August 2018).

Boren, K., et al. "Electromyographic Analysis of Gluteus Medius and Gluteus Maximus During Rehabilitation Exercises," *International Journal of Sports Physical Therapy* 6:3 (September 2011).

Donnelly, Joseph M. et al. (eds.). *Travell, Simons & Simons' Myofascial Pain and Dysfunction: The Trigger Point Manual* Third Edition (Alphen aan den Rijn, The Netherlands: Wolters Kluwer), 2018.

Ergun, T., and H. Lakadamyali. "CT and MRI in the evaluation of extraspinal sciatica," *The British Journal of Radiology* 83:993 (September 2010).

Garner, Ginger. *Medical Therapeutic Yoga: Biopsychosocial Rehabilitation and Wellness Care* (Pencaitland, East Lothian, UK: Handspring Publishing Limited), 2016.

Louw, Adriaan. *Why Do I Hurt? A Patient Book About the Neuroscience of Pain* (Minneapolis: Orthopedic Physical Therapy Products), 2013.

Major, N.M., and C.A. Helms. "MR Imaging of the Knee: Findings in Asymptomatic Collegiate Basketball Players," *American Journal of Roentgenology* 179:3 (September 2002).

McMakin C., Walter M. Gregory, and Terry M. Phillips. "Cytokine Changes with Microcurrent Treatment of Fibromyalgia Associated with Cervical Trauma," *Journal of Bodywork and Movement Therapies* 9:3 (July 2005).

Milgrom, C., et al. "Rotator-cuff Changes in Asymptomatic Adults. The Effect of Age, Hand Dominance and Gender," *The Journal of Bone & Joint Surgery* 77:2 (March 1995).

Murphy, LB, et al. "One in Four People May Develop Symptomatic Hip Osteoarthritis in His or Her Lifetime," *Osteoarthritis and Cartilage* 18:11 (November 2010).

Myers, Thomas W. *Anatomy Trains: Myofascial Meridians for Manual and Movement Therapists* (London: Churchill Livingstone), 2014.

Register, B. et al. "Prevalence of Abnormal Hip Findings in Asymptomatic Participants: A Prospective, Blinded Study," *American Journal of Sports Medicine* 40:12 (December 2012).

Riddle, D.L., et al. "Use of a Validated Algorithm to Judge the Appropriateness of Total Knee Arthroplasty in the United States: A Multicenter Longitudinal Cohort Study," *Arthritis & Rheumatology* 66:8 (August 2014).

Seegers, J.C., C.A. Engelbrecht, and D.H. van Papendorp. "Activation of Signal-Transduction Mechanisms May Underlie the Therapeutic Effects of an Applied Electric Field," *Medical Hypotheses* 57:2 (August 2005).

RESOURCES

Looking for the products mentioned in this book? You can find the exact links on how and where to purchase these items on my website at christinekoth.com/resources

Hip Hook - TheHipHook.com to purchase the Hip Hook and for tips on positions to release the iliacus.

4" ball

Calming app

Foam roller

Meditation cushion

Orthotics

Kinesiotape

Shoes with good arch supports

SI brace

Standing desk

GET HELP

Find a chiropractor and physical therapist - Search the web for "physical therapist near me" or "chiropractor near me."

Find a FSM practitioner
https://frequencyspecific.com/frequency-specific-microcurrent-practitioners/

Find a functional medicine doctor (a medical doctor that identifies and treats the root causes of disease)
www.ifm.org/find-a-practitioner/

Find a naturopathic doctor
www.naturopathic.org

CONTINUE ON YOUR
HEALING JOURNEY

Use the code BOOKPERKS for an exclusive readers discount off the Hip Hook and the Hip Flexor Release Ball.

Scan Here

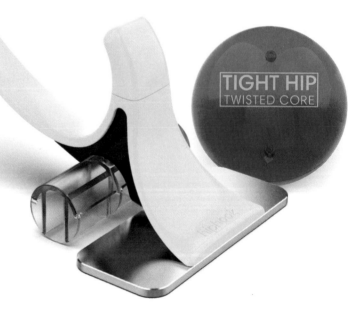

Don't forget to download your free exercise handout at **TightHipTwistedCore.com/ReadersGift** and check out exercise videos and explanations at **AlethaHealth.com**